the MYSTICAL MARRIAGE

Gerhard Wehr
teaches at the Diakonenschule
in Rummelsberg bei
Nuremberg and is a
distinguished writer on
Christian spirituality, depth
psychology and anthroposophy,
with many works to his name,
including biographies of Martin
Buber, Rudolf Steiner and
C. G. Jung.

The MYSTICAL MARRIAGE

Symbol and Meaning of the Human Experience

GERHARD WEHR

**Translated from the German
by
JILL SUTCLIFFE**

First UK edition 1990
First published in German as
Heilige Hochzeit: Symbol und Erfahrung menschlichen Reifung

© Kösel-Verlag GmbH & Co., Munich 1986
English translation © The Aquarian Press 1990

British Library Cataloguing in Publication Data

Wehr, Gerhard
The mystical marriage
1. Marriage. Religious viewpoint
I. Title. II. Heilige Hochzeit — English
291'.1'783581

ISBN 1-85274-060-4

*Crucible is an imprint of the Aquarian Press,
part of the Thorsons Publishing Group, Wellingborough,
Northamptonshire, NN8 2RQ, England*

Printed in Great Britain by Woolnough Bookbinding Limited,
Irthlingborough, Northamptonshire
Typesetting by MJL Limited, Hitchin, Hertfordshire

1 3 5 7 9 10 8 6 4 2

For Else

I wish to thank the Klopstock-Foundation in Hamburg
for supporting my work
G.W.

The archetype of Hieros Gamos *marks a high-point of the human race and of the individual human being as a symbol of the creative union of opposites.*

—Erich Neumann

Great is the mystery of marriage ... People provide the world's continuance. But their continuance involves the partnership of marriage. Let us recognize the undefiled partnership, for it is possessed of great power!
—The Gospel according to Philip, 60

Mysterium coniunctionis *is a human concern. It is the* nymphagogos *(handmaiden) of heavenly marriage. How can a man distance himself from this event?*
—C. G. Jung to Erich Neumann, 1952

CONTENTS

Introduction

Human beings have deep desires, some expressed, others left unspoken, which are set against their fears and anxieties. People are disturbed not only by what the future may bring but also by what is happening today. No detailed list is required: any newspaper will contain all sorts of examples. But it is not just external facts that lie behind our fears and worries. Both worry and desire lie at the root of human existence, in man's soul. Every single person experiences and suffers from them.

In this book we take one aspect of this universal experience and discuss it from different angles. What is more unbearable than to feel isolated, spiritually torn, incomplete and alienated even from oneself? What is more blessed than to overcome this discord through the harmony of togetherness, in the healing state of you-and-me, in the happy union of those once separated? This 'spiritual longing' is at once the hope of mankind and the individual's dream. Even in light-hearted gossip about one's 'dream man' or 'dream woman' there is a faint echo of this longing. That a couple should 'click' has been an ever-recurring theme for singers, story-tellers, poets and playwrights throughout the ages. *Marriage* is the perfect model, the means of overcoming loneliness and ending one's inner isolation. In fairy tales the much desired prince dreams of marriage with a bride who seems unobtainable, yet whom fate has destined to be his. And what are these fairy tales but magic mirrors reflecting our own love quest, highlighting and illustrating it through the most ancient of pictures and symbols? Free from the bonds of time or space, myths and fairy tales can speak to us with astonishing directness. It is as if there is a secret correspondence between their form and content and the depths of our own souls. They are addressed to an area of the unconscious which lies beyond our personal experience, even beyond what we have forgotten or suppressed. Dreams also illustrate this point, in that by involving us in puzzling references or incidents, they put us in conscious touch with a far-reaching, neglected, transpersonal dimension of spiritual reality. The business of psychoanalysis is to unlock the symbols of dreams and myths so that the individual can understand and accept them with a qualitative widening of his awareness. This encourages spiritual growth, a maturing of the personality and a rounding off of the whole man. In the same way the symbol of marriage can be understood as expressing this wholeness. Opposite poles come together: male and female, light and dark, inner and outer . . .

To be clear about the significance of symbols in modern life it can be helpful to go back in time and examine our spiritual and religious tradition. This is where true signs and symbols, which are part of a collective unconscious, are hidden, and they can always set free meaning for the individual. *Mystical marriage* is such a symbol, a hieroglyph that needs interpreting for the individual, not least because it is connected with specialized subsidiary themes of religio-spiritual history. At first sight it seems remote from modern preoccupations. For one thing, present-day references are hard to come by. It is also undeniable that co-operative research from different points of view is needed, if the material available in symbolic form and its underlying implications is to be treated really adequately. At the same time the central theme of mystical marriage is closely constrained, and not only by the historical facts of religion and myth. Spiritual and intellectual growth and the human factor are always to be taken into account. It is not just outworn superstitions we have to discuss, but man's future destiny. Mere accumulation of scholarly knowledge is not enough for this. There needs to be active participation in the powerfully magnetic field of symbolism, even though the outline of a particular myth was given meaning long, long ago.

As a symbol, mystical marriage has implications beyond its immediate meaning. Such authentic symbols have enormous positive potential for vitality and power. They are not just pretty pictures; rather, using allegorical sign language, they convey meaning at many different levels. Even without considering their possible further implications[1] we have to remember that a living symbol is immediately pregnant with meaning. It is *pregnant* compared to what we expect from precisely defined, practical symbols such as traffic signs, or those indicating technical measurements, etc. Instead of giving a precise direction or producing a reflex action, as is necessary in modern technology and communication, an authentic symbol has a qualitatively different function. It stands for depth, multidimensionality, and fullness of meaning, and resists tidy definition. And definition of such a symbol is at best of a provisional nature. Different aspects or layers of meaning can of course be distinguished, but the essential core meaning of a true symbol remains an enigma. At the same time it can continue to form the basis of new interpretations of symbolic meaning. One has only to think of the many figurative objects in religious ceremonies, such as water, bread, wine, etc. Again and again, on ceremonial occasions or in personal meditation, they manifest their spiritual power, which is unaffected either by rational criticism or by theological exegesis.

It is true that codes have been devised to explain mysteries such as mystical marriage. But the quintessence — the *mysterium coniunctionis* or secret of becoming 'one' — remains hidden, at least for the uninvolved spectator concerned only with his 'objectivity' and keeping a distance. Access is possible only through initiation,[2] consummation and wholehearted participation. To draw a parallel: what is a description of love when compared with the act of loving or being loved! Let us listen to Novalis's *Hymn*:

> Few know
> The secret of love,
> Feel its insatiability
> And eternal thirst.
> The divine meaning
> Of Holy Communion
> Is an enigma to earthly reasoning . . .

That is the voice of someone 'in the know', who can say of himself that 'his eyes have been opened/That he has measured/The unfathomable depths of heaven'. It is the voice of one present at the critical moment, when the deepest reality associated with mystical marriage has been manifested. The youthful Novalis shows signs here of his experience as an initiate, as a practitioner.

And this much should be said at the outset: we can speak

of a *'mysterium' coniunctionis* and of a 'mystical' marriage because
more is meant than the human level of an I-and-you relationship. The 'eternal Other' (Martin Buber) is always involved.
An interpersonal relationship will be experienced fully, or even
just be glimpsed or sensed as a possibility, only in the context
of the eternal.

There are two basic experiences closely bound up with
human activity and make-up. One has to do with the fact that
man does not live in perfect harmony either with himself or
with his fellows. We have only to think of the painful experience
of antagonism, of argument, of alienation — in religious terms,
man's need for redemption — to realize this. On the other hand,
human beings long to be delivered from this unhappy state of
affairs. This has been at the heart of hope since time began.
Connected with it is a longing for identity, wholeness and harmony. And as individuals seek to overcome their own inner
divisions, so mankind as a whole, faced with a deadly threat
to existence, longs for peace and an end to self-destructive conflict. This does not mean the removal of all differences. Life-
creating opposites are necessary. But the *mysterium coniunctionis*
is a mystery of reconciliation. This covers a wide span of meaning. It reaches from the first cry of the newborn child, whose
first wish is to feel comfortable on this planet, to the cry from
the Cross: 'Thy will be done!' — the expression of final fulfilment. It reaches also from the inner attachment and mutual
mental, spiritual and physical intercourse of two lovers, to a
sacramental or mystical marriage, the divine essence of which
(as Novalis says) remains an enigma to mere earthly reasoning.

What has been said so far is acceptable as part of a general
introduction. But the secret core of mystical marriage will be
fully revealed only if it can be looked at from different angles.
And yet at the same time mere knowledge of facts or outward
appearances will take us only a little way. Full knowledge of
the mystery requires active, living participation.

1

Aspects of Mystical Marriage in Comparative Religion

Hieros Gamos, or mystical marriage, is a concept that was widely known in oriental and Graeco-Roman antiquity,[1] but the subject itself is nevertheless shrouded in mystery. Countless myths exist in which god and goddess, as well as god and human, celebrate marriage. In this context the psychoanalyst Erich Neumann describes mythology as being invariably 'the instinctive portrayal of self in parallel key events of human existence, and important for the very reason that it enables us to draw on an unadulterated stock of human experience, since the statements it makes are unclouded by self-conscious knowledge.'[2]

Human experience of earthly marriage and the individual's own awareness of what is godly and divine interact with one another. It is precisely this additional material-spiritual dimension at the centre of mystical marriage that makes it a religious celebration and carries mankind to the very heart of all that we associate with divine worship. So, quoting Ulrich Mann, we may put forward the fundamental proposition that:

While there is pairing in the animal kingdom, and the legal ceremony of marriage is for the most part a matter only of official registration, yet wedlock in its innermost essence is something mystical, one might say, something holy. 'Hieros Gamos' contains the idea that it is the ritual fulfilment of a divine wedding celebration. When children play at weddings it is always in the spirit of fairy stories, with a shining hero and a king's daughter. 'Till-death-us-do-part' happy endings are based on the solemn truth that fundamentally holy matrimony has no end, but is an everlasting celebration — for everything in the sight of God is eternal.[3]

One could go on to say that whenever ritual takes place or is represented in mythical form, we are in effect participating in the eternal; and the message of ritual contains deeper value than everyday communication which merely satisfies the need for information. The question arises here, to what extent and in what way is mystical marriage of any concern to contemporary men and women, and how far is it relevant to our particular circumstances? First let us consider some facts that should facilitate our approach.

To begin with, there is the age-old fertility myth which has been celebrated since the beginning of human thought and religious observance. This is no figment of the imagination created or dreamt up by human beings. For those who know how mystical feeling is bound up with worship this myth is a psychophysical reality with the characteristics of the divine. Its two aspects are inseparable. Human life and human actions are all related to the existence and activities of the gods themselves. Birth, marriage and death all stem from a dynamic force which casts its influence over mankind and enters deeply into human experience. These aspects of life are controlled by the gods. According to Walter F. Otto, 'It is not just that ideas based on superstition exert a certain power. Here there is genuine procreation, here immortal forms develop, here mankind is being regenerated.'[4]

It is an almighty, creative god, then, with the power to govern the heavens, who joins himself to a profusely abundant earth goddess at the beginning of a new year. Spring and the New Year become the fixed seasons for the recurrence of mystical marriage. And simply because the original myth is not an arbitrary fantasy or the product of some prehistoric entertainment industry, but the ennoblement of human existence by a higher level of being, it follows that man's observance of ritual is as though it is a gift from the gods — not just an empty exercise. The myth merits 'celebratory conduct and performance, lifting man to a higher sphere' (W.F. Otto) and this, moreover, in the midst of his everyday preoccupations. It is through myth and ritual that human existence first acquires order and meaning. What people do in their everyday lives, as in their religious observance — the basis for their decision-making — is laid down from 'above'. The critical decisions of human life are in this category.

Seen from this angle, there is special significance in the revelation of man's divine origin: 'We are *God's* children.' Man discovers the archetype and pattern for his own life in the marriage of the gods and the communion of gods and goddesses. This does not mean that man should project his fears and hopes through an imaginary screen to a world 'on the other side'. It is much truer to say that man himself is a 'projection' of God, and not least at the very roots of his existence, that is, in his sexuality. For this reason, according to Julius Evola, early man sought to base the secret and the essence of his own sexuality on the creative polarity of the divine:

The sexes existed as abstract powers and principles before they had any physical existence; before they appeared in 'natural' form they held sway in the mystical, cosmic, spiritual, supernatural sphere. Man sought to comprehend the nature of the eternal-masculine and eternal-feminine by comparison with the sexually-differentiated gods and goddesses, of whom the opposite sexes of humanity are but a reflection and a particular manifestation.[5]

And how many different reflections of this kind there are!

The ancient Chinese *yin-yang* sign is the paramount symbol of this cosmic relationship:

Here a dynamic unity is graphically realized in a classical form. For *yang* (the creative, luminous, masculine, etc.) and *yin* (the conceiving, dark, feminine, etc.) are so closely interlocked and bound to each other, that together they form a rounded whole. The surrounding circle stands for Tao, the all-embracing (though a single word cannot fully define it) in which the polarity of *yin-yang* is literally reconciled without, however, being neutralized. So, despite (or because of) this paradox, we can see the *yin-yang* symbol as an aspect of mystical marriage. Those who wish to become followers of Tao must (in the spirit of Lao Tse) recognize their manhood and protect their womanhood in order to be 'the river-bed of the world'. The dynamic interaction between *yin* and *yang* finds not only its graphic but also its practical expression in the *I Ching*, that ancient book of prophecy and wisdom. On the one hand its famous 64 hexagram variations of *yang* (male) are shown as unbroken lines $\equiv$, and those of *yin* (female) as broken lines $\equiv\equiv$. On the other hand the present-day user of this Chinese method of fortune-telling with coins or the yarrow plant is in touch with a duality which personally affects him and his current situation.[6] It is surprising that it is only in our day that it has been pointed out that this *yin–yang* symbolism represents a basic natural law as well as a 'hidden key to life'. Martin Schönberger had drawn an analogy between this ancient Chinese book of wisdom and the genetic code of modern natural science.[7]

Now, as then, we are dealing with the mystery of life itself. We should remember too that the viewpoint and experience of agricultural peoples was first-hand: it was rain from heaven that made 'Mother Earth' fertile, a clear demonstration of creative Nature. There are linguistic parallels in this field also, as for example in ancient Greek where to sow (*speirein*) and to plough (*aroun*) also stand for 'to beget'. There are also traditions in which Mother Earth is able to give birth alone, without a creative partner. According to Hesiod, the Earth (Gaia) gave birth to the Sky (Uranus) so that according to heavenly genealogy he became a separate being. 'He then completely covered the Earth', thus joining her in marriage, that is, for all time. The myth tells us that Uranus and Gaia, by consummating mystical marriage, enabled life to develop. The fruitfulness of Mother Earth is a cosmic prototype of fruitfulness in general.

The cosmic myth whereby the god of Heaven and the goddess of Earth join in mystical marriage is widespread. 'It is found', Mircea Eliade tells us, 'above all in Oceania — from Indonesia to Micronesia — but also in Asia, Africa and in both the Americas.'[8] Basically this cosmic union is found in all unsophisticated early agricultural communities. It appears in the religious history of the ancient Orient as well as in Graeco-Roman antiquity. In Mesopotamia at New Year the king is joined in matrimony with a priestess. As an incarnation of Astarte or Ishtar, the mother goddess, she will ensure that fresh crops will grow and that the fields will bear their expected harvest.

The mother goddess Astarte is the helpmate of Tammuz, a character dogged by fate. For every year he must descend into the Kingdom of the Dead. Death for him is inevitable. But Astarte follows her young husband and, reciting all his honours and dignities, calls him back to life. Together they celebrate mystical marriage. The fruit of their union is the renewed abundance of the valley of the Euphrates. But the victory of the mighty god Marduk over the power of chaos, embodied in the god Tamat, is also celebrated. Mystical marriage forms a part of this New Year festival too. King and priestess, representing the gods, meet in a chamber in a ziggurat, thereby fulfilling the need to foster the well-being of the whole countryside.[9]

In the ancient Assyrian pantheon, Anath, the virgin, the 'sister', is assigned as companion to Baal, the fertility and weather god. Here too myths of the natural world, of procreation and growth, of ripening and death, are closely linked to *Hieros Gamos*.

One of the best-known pairs of gods and goddesses are Isis and Osiris from the eastern delta of the Nile. Not only as an embodiment of the rejuvenating power of the waters of the Nile, but also as Lord of Death and Rebirth, the murdered Osiris binds himself mystically to his grieving sister-bride. For as Isis bends over the mummified body of Osiris she conceives Horus, the divine child,[10] whose gaze unites sun and moon, a redeeming look which will renew the earth and mankind itself. The later Isis-Osiris (or Serapis) mysteries, which were to acquire great significance for ancient Greece, show us that it was not just renewal of the earth, fertility of the fields, or an abundance of children that was intended. It is said of Osiris that he brought the Egyptians out of their primitive state, turned them away from cannibalism, and established the rule of law; thus he is recognized as a bringer of civilization. Why should he be so honoured? Erich Neumann has an answer to this question:

Because he is not only a god of fertility in the sense of natural growth. His creativity embraces this level, but is not restricted to it. Every bringer of civilization is a successful synthesis of the conscious and the creative unconscious. He has reached a creative centre *within himself* [my italic], a centre of renewal and rebirth, as symbolized in the fertility rituals of New Year festivals, identifying with the creative godhead, and on which the world's existence depends. The ritual and the human aspect combine *in him*. . . The ritual is concerned not just with preserving nature but with achieving mastery over nature, through an analogous creative centre in man. Finding the treasure is impossible unless the hero finds his soul and sets free his own female attributes — receptiveness, invention, creativity. . .[11]

In terms of modern psychoanalysis, this has given us a key to understanding the myth of mystical marriage and its ritual as a process to be followed by each individual. In particular the ancient Elusinian and Dionysian mysteries, not forgetting the cults of Adonis and Attis, lend themselves to this interpretation. What the myth tells us is that the core of the mystery — what is purifying, enlightening and at one with the godhead — is active participation in it, experienced through it and *in* it. It goes *itself* 'to the very frontier of life and death'; it crosses 'Proserpine's threshold' as it is called in Apuleius's richly revealing fantasy, *The Golden Ass* (Chapter 11). It also takes in the 'midnight sun' whose incandescent light shows the way for the initiated to the gods above as well as to those below.[12]

Of course we hear of more marriages among the gods. There is Zeus, the Indo-European god of sky and weather, bound in mystical marriage with goddesses and mortal women alike. There is Dionysus, who marries Ariadne on the island of Naxos. Hesiod, Homer, Virgil and other classical authors describe their Olympian heroes and show in legend how they can be taken as 'a model for human union'.[13] So there is running through the conscious history of mankind a corresponding inner consequence, that the cosmically significant event that enables the womb of Earth to be productive leads more and more to an *individual* experience. The sacred bridal chamber (*conubium*) of king or priest and priestess is not restricted to them alone, for in the mysteries there are always initiates, albeit a strictly limited number, who cross the threshold of understanding and enlightenment. Yet the mysteries allow even novices to experience mystical death. The great significance of ancient Greek and oriental myths for the history of religion, as perceived by Mircea Eliade, is that they 'make one aware of the need for a personal religious experience that will last throughout the whole of life, that is, in Christian terms, including "salvation" in eternity. Such a *personal* religious experience could not be developed in the framework of public ritual . . .'. But the initiation themes live on, bound up with tradition; they become more and more *intense*; they take on quite new practical qualities, the experience of those who see renewal not only in the seasons and external natural phenomena but are *themselves* absorbed in a process of renewal. Eliade continues:

An archaic scenario therefore lends itself to being taken up again and adapted for many and various purposes, from *unio mystica* [mystical marriage] with the godhead to magical mastery over mortality or the attainment of final liberation — of Nirvana. It is as though initiation scenarios were bound up inextricably with the innermost forms of spiritual life and as though initiation was absolutely essential for every attempt at total renewal, every effort to transcend the normal natural condition of mankind in order to reach a holy state of being.[14]

Such conclusions, of course, need documentary support. Although the mysteries were known about in general terms, any unveiling of them by initiates carried heavy penalties. What really happened at Eleusis or in the cult of Attis, what the celebrants and initiates experienced and what mysterious rites took place are questions that have been debated since time immemorial, and are naturally controversial. At least fragments of these secret liturgies have been handed down to us. But our authorities, early Christian writers, were certainly not reporting in order to give us factual information about these practices, but to condemn them. This creates a problem for the rites in question, whether they are concerned with mystical death and rebirth on the one hand, or with mystical marriage and procreation on the other.

The initiates obviously learned nothing new; there was no extension of knowledge. There are many indications that the basic myth was already known. The so-called secret rules were not mentioned to neophytes, let alone 'taught'. There were, however, ritual gestures which typified the mystery, and there were holy objects that could be seen and even touched. The form of rituals has been passed on in *Protreptikos* [Exhortation] II.21.2, by St Clement of Alexandria, who, judging by the many references in his writings, must have had knowledge of many details relating to the mysteries:[15]

I have fasted; I have drunk the *Kykeon* [cup]; I have taken [it] from the large basket, touched it and put it in the little basket, then taken it again and put it back in the large basket.

An apparently trivial gesture, but for the participants a holy act, for its association with an unnamed ritual object — either a ritual phallus, if, as some have suggested, it involves mystical marriage to a god; or the representation of a female organ if, according to another hypothesis, it involves not wedlock but divine childbirth as part of the myth.[16] But does one meaning exclude the other in such a deeply symbolic ceremony? The human linked to God becomes in sacred terms 'God's child', the reborn, a new person. Mystical marriage and rebirth are two aspects of the same mystery. The proximity in time of *Hieros Gamos* and the proclamation of a joyful rebirth, gives colour to such an interpretation. Given the difficulty of source material we must keep an open mind within a wide range of interpretations, also taking into account that the fragments handed down are of relatively late date and come from different mysteries and different regions. However, time and again the theme of *Heiros Gamos* is, if not positively central, either implied or at least mentioned. Let us take another fragment. It comes from the pen of St Hippolytus of Rome who, through his writings, took part in the controversies about heresy that engaged the church at the turn of the second and third centuries. In this connection he records the chant of the priests of Eleusis, who would call out during the nocturnal ritual:

Sublime Brimo bore a Holy One, a son of Brimo, strongest of the strong. Noble is such heavenly birth on high, strong indeed is one so born!

Here again we have cryptic words which, in their totality, like the mysteries themselves, require research into important problems. We know that the second level of initiation encompasses the so-called *Epopteia,* in which the participant in the mystery becomes an *epopt,* one who sees. 'Seeing' here is not at all the same as seeing with one's eyes. The epopt must prove his special power of vision when the torch in the *telesterion* (holy place) is extinguished and the priest steps forward with a casket. The priest opens it and takes out the key symbol of Eleusis, an ear of corn. According to Walter F. Otto:

There is no doubt about the miraculous nature of events. The ear of corn, which grows and ripens with miraculous speed, is part of the mysteries of the agricultural goddess Demeter, just as the vine growing in a few hours is part of the festival of Dionysus... We find the same in the ceremonies of more primitive peoples, a plant of surpassing wonder.[17]

Soon after this, *Hieros Gamos* is celebrated between a priest and a priestess of Demeter. The ancient myth, once concerned with field rites and fertility, becomes an unseen influence which grips and affects each individual differently.

Even if the whole liturgy of the mysteries were in our possession in the form of an order of service, what is communicable is not the particulars but the fearful yet blessed nature of the ceremonial, the numinous experience of the holy drama. Only thus is it understandable that the initiates of old could endorse the sense of the hymn to Demeter: 'Happy are those earth-dwellers who have seen these things. In the dark kingdom of the shades, very different is the fate of the initiated and the uninitiated.' Pindar says the same in his expression of faith: 'Happy the man who has seen this before he descends beneath the earth! He knows the purpose of life! He also knows its beginning.' We gather from a text known as the *Rites of Mithras*[18] that this 'vision' corresponds to an inner change of attitude. Among other things this text declares '. . . and after this man who is called out of so many thousands to immortality is created by you [god] today . . .' and 'Born through the birth that begets this life, I shall be set free in death.'[19]

Other witnesses speak of a self-confidence which gives initiates a likeness to the god. Whoever has been present at the wedding of god and goddess in a holy shrine and returned with a new enriched life from the 'other side of Proserpine's threshold', will appreciate these lines of Firmicus Maternus:

> Have trust in the mysteries!
> As god saves,
> So salvation for us
> Grows out of suffering.

Finally Apuleius has preserved a prayer of thanksgiving from a mystery which Rudolf Bultmann considered an example of Isis-worship in which the Egypto-Greek mother goddess was invoked in a way very reminiscent of early Christian worship of the Virgin Mary.[20] Mircea Eliade sums it up:

A spiritual rebirth is involved, a regeneration expressed in a fundamental change in the celebrant's existing way of life. Thanks to the initiation the neophyte attains another level of being: he becomes like the gods, identifies himself with the gods. Apotheosis, deification, immortality (*apathanatismos*) are concepts with which all Greek mystics were familiar.[21]

From this it does not require too great a step to carry over to early Christianity images from the Greek world or mysteries: union with God, betrothal and marriage — above all if it can be guaranteed that sexual elements will not be involved in mystical marriage — a task to which ecclesiastical writers of the first century AD devoted themselves with great (not to say too great) enthusiasm.

However, a full transition from the symbols of the ancient world selected here to thoughts of mystical marriage in Christianity is not possible until we have examined the Old Testament for possible hints or references.

2

Mystical Marriage in the Old Testament

Before we examine how symbols of mystical marriage appear in the Bible, in the Old Testament first of all, we should look briefly at the background of religious history.

Given the geographical location of the Holy Land and its association with early Eastern culture, we can understand that its Canaanite inhabitants must have shared the early religious traditions of the death, rebirth, and marriage of the gods. Close neighbourly relations between Israel and the indigenous Canaanites, even though the latter served other gods, indicate that an early and active religio-cultural exchange took place. Moreover it is apparent that there was much contact with the culture of the Nile valley, and more with that of the land between the rivers Tigris and Euphrates. Especially during the troubled times in which the prophets Isaiah and Hosea, then Jeremiah and Ezekiel, were active (i.e. between 800 and 900 BC), violent clashes were reported between Israelite adherents of Jehovah and Canaanite worshippers of Baal. This struggle between Jehovah and Baal took place in the very midst of the people of Israel. The Israelite prophets fought passionately for the souls of their people, with admonition, preaching and pastoral care, telling them that they would lose their religion, their political identity and their integrity if they lost their belief in the Lord Jehovah.

Baal, the principal Canaanite deity, was always a localized god, restricted to a particular place. He looked after the wel-fare and protection of one area.[1] He was the same Baal who, together with Astarte, was responsible for the fertility of one country and its people. Jehovah, on the other hand, was a migratory deity, a travelling companion, a God who accom-panied His 'wandering people'. Baal's territoriality went hand

in hand with the power of renewal and greening of the land.
Neither man nor animal nor the earth could thrive without
him. If he did not return, year after year, the summer drought
would continue instead of the natural world being revived. The
restriction of this god to his territory made possible a cult
characterized by emphasis on vegetal-sexual symbolism. The
climax of his annual death and rebirth culminated in the mystical marriage celebrated on New Year's Day by king and queen,
chief priest and priestess, and it was this that guaranteed the
life of the locality and the whole region.

Whereas Baal was part of the natural course of the seasons,
Jehovah, the God of Israel, was known as the ever-present, face-
to-face God[2] who, as the 'Good Shepherd' (see Psalm 23) had
led His people since the days of the patriarchs, the flight from
Egypt and the historic wandering in the desert. However, Baal's
and Astarte's attraction must have been particularly strong if
one takes into account on the one hand the words of warning
and prophecy, and on the other the promises with which the
prophets Isaiah, Jeremiah and Hosea sought to brighten the
image of Jehovah in Israel. The main effect was to direct attention away from the myths and rites of the mystical marriage
of alien gods — the prophets declared such marriage to be
unlawful 'adultery' — and thereby they sought to put an end
to the backsliding of the Chosen People. But were Jehovah's
messengers successful in keeping the image and idea of mystical marriage away from their people?

Experience shows that a living symbol, that is to say one
vibrant with life, will be stronger than any rational argument
that might be put into the field against it. In the long run, especially where an agricultural way of life and local customs are
dominant, it does not cease to be influential — it may be the
'dynamic symbol'. Existing symbols may even be imbued with
new meaning. So in Israel the question was whether the cult
of mystical marriage could be harmonized with belief in God.

To begin with there is much evidence that the symbol of mystical marriage found its way into Israel. This is not just to say
that borrowings were made from heathen, non-Israelite
sources. Of course time and again, where religions conflict or
where one 'proselytizes' the other, there are such borrowings.
One can trace points of contact, possibilities of assimilation
and finally of integration.

However, it is not a question only of a (so to speak) horizontal permeation assimilating an alien belief, but of a *vertical* permeation process. Genuine symbols cannot be gauged exclusively by the way they have been passed on or adopted from the outside. They have their roots in a superpersonal, archetypal ground — what C. G. Jung called the collective unconscious. From these depths symbols may appear spontaneously, as though self-created, just as we can be haunted by visions of unusual things about which we have previously known nothing. It also requires an inner readiness to accept something *supposedly* new and unfamiliar, before an outside idea can be adopted and finally integrated.

For our purposes this means that marriage and holy matrimony are manifestations of such an archetype: that of the union of opposites. And the ancient twelve tribes of Israel are no exception. We see the orgiastic cult of Canaanite society follow such a transformation. Many Old Testament witnesses testify how wearisome and strewn with obstacles was the path to that end. Here are some examples.

First marriage was already firmly embedded in the life of early Israel, because man was created as male *and* female (Genesis 1:26f.) and also because the patriarchs from the beginning took great care over the choice of wives and the marriage of their children. So when he was in ripe old age Abraham made his oldest servant swear a solemn oath that his son Isaac would 'not take a wife of the daughters of the Canaanites (Genesis 24:3) but would go on a journey to seek a bride. Marriage and the birth of a male heir provide the key dates in ancient genealogy (Genesis 5). Marriage in the Old Testament may have been arranged but it was not lacking in erotic love and affection between the partners. Consequently adultery was severely punished: it was considered a characteristic of the pagan world. When Abimelech, King of Gerar, coveted Sarah, Abraham's wife, and had her seized, he was threatened in a dream with death, 'for she is a man's wife' (Genesis 20:3).

If adultery broke God's commandment, and thereby represented a serious offence against God's covenant with His people, then even more taking part in heathen fertility rites was a crime worthy of death, and one incriminating not just the individual but the whole race.

So it was this view of adultery that moved the prophets to see signs that the people of the covenant had become apostate breakers of their faith, inasmuch as they sacrificed to other gods and took part in Baal-Tammuz's mystical marriage rites. The religious importance of adultery arose from the fact that Jehovah himself had entered into marriage with His people Israel. Thus He had joined with them in mystical marriage long before, even though the making of the covenant on Mount Sinai had not then been depicted in the images and parables of holy matrimony. More was involved than a simple 'law-giving'; more than accepting duties and rights in modern legal terms. This is why the prophets repeatedly refer to a conjugal communion of love between God and His people Israel, the bride or virgin, as she is frequently called — for example in Isaiah 37:22, Jeremiah 31:4 and 21, and Amos 5:2. And Hosea (2:19f.) puts these words into Jehovah's mouth:

And I will betroth thee unto me for ever; yea, I will betroth thee unto me in righteousness and in judgment and in loving kindness and in mercies I will even betroth thee unto me in faithfulness: and thou shalt know the Lord.[3]

Earlier in his speech the followers of Baal are condemned for their *unholy* alliance (Hosea 2:8-17). It is divine love alone that can form a lasting basis for a new relationship. As it says in the book of Isaiah (54:5-7):

For thy Maker is thine husband; the Lord of hosts is his name; and thy Redeemer the Holy One of Israel; The God of the whole earth shall he be called. For the Lord hath called thee as a woman forsaken and grieved in spirit, and a wife of youth when thou wast refused, saith thy God.

To talk about marriage between Jehovah and Israel is therefore neither an arbitrary nor accidental metaphor, but rather a well-established symbol of union between God and His people. And because it is a living symbol, and its meaning becomes evident in a practical situation or event, so this extraordinary command is given to the prophet Hosea:

And the Lord said to Hosea. Go, take unto thee a wife of whoredoms and children of whoredoms: for the land hath committed great whoredom, departing from the Lord. (Hosea 1:2).

This means that God's messenger is so involved with the inner life of the tribe that his own marriage must mirror the unfaithfulness between Jehovah and his adulterous bride, the strumpet Israel. While this prophetic utterance anticipates God's action in a visionary and allegorical way, the symbolism of marriage that we find in Hosea uncovers the reality of Israel's backsliding and infidelity. The final purpose of the prophet's message, however, is to show that Jehovah is ever-loving and in spite of infidelity and adultery will not leave His people in the lurch but will continue in a loving relationship — in contrast to the Canaanite bridegroom on the hills and under the green trees of Palestine.

What would happen though if the prophet were fortunate enough to suppress the singing, dancing and dissolute practices in honour of Baal and Astaroth for all time? Would this be the end of all mystical marriage practices? This can hardly be so, for Israel's divine worship lives in word and song in the Psalms. And one of these poetic psalms is entitled 'A Song of loves' (Psalm 45). It sings of the wedding of a king and his bride:

My heart is inditing a good matter:
I speak of the things which I have made
Touching the King...
Thou are fairer than the children of men:
Grace is poured unto thy lips...
Kings' daughters were among thy honourable women:
Upon thy right hand did stand the queen
In gold of Ophir.

Another book of the Old Testament, also a collection of songs, speaks more frankly. Nowhere in the Bible does the theme of mystical marriage resound more expressively, joyfully, and ardently than in the Song of Solomon, the 'Song of Songs'. After the prayer 'Out of the Depths' (Psalm 130) and the solemn hymns of the Psalms or 'Book of Praises', the Bible-reader is surprised to come upon an elated, indeed impassioned, lovesong which (scarcely veiled in simile and metaphor) celebrates the physical charms of young lovers. The fathers of Old Testament canonical law must have had a 'problem' in deciding whether this section of the Book of Books could be so organized and interpreted as to make the Song of Songs suitable for reading at the Feast of the Passover. The early rabbis did see to it that no-one under thirty, then the age of maturity, saw these scrolls. Was this early censorship of Bible literature which might be 'inimical to youth'? Needless to say, one should not apply the moral standards of recent bourgeois times to the Judea of the first half-century BC or even earlier. So what is it all about?

A number of possible interpretations of the practices of church and synagogue have been debated over a long period. Two interpretations above all confront one another. One sees in the Song of Songs a cycle of old folk-songs or of dramatic anthems such as might have been sung or performed at rural festivals, for example at Israelite village weddings. The other opposing interpretation saw a new basic meaning in this erotic song of love: the erotic allusions and comparisons were intended to glorify the love of Jehovah for His people, 'The Virgin Israel'. It was this interpretation that the fathers of Old Testament canonical law adopted when, at the rabbinical synod of Jamnia in AD 100, it had to be decided whether the text could be accepted (as it was, in fact) as belonging to the Holy Scriptures.

We know how Christendom dealt with it. Just as the rabbis skirted round the literal meaning to apply it to Jehovah and Israel, so the Church saw in it Christ's love for his bride, the community. Finally there is the view that the Song of Songs refers to the 'great mystery' of love, of which St Paul speaks (Ephesians 5 passim, esp. 32). This symbolic interpretation has been generally accepted by the Church for centuries. It was already in vogue when the second Ecumenical Council of Constantinople in AD 553 solemnly vetoed the view that the Song of Songs was simply a collection of popular songs about love and marriage. If anyone contradicted the Council's decision — for example the Greek theologian Theodore of Mopsuestia (d. AD 428) — he was threatened with excommunication. Medieval mysticism (to anticipate a later chapter) made this symbolic meaning its own, spearheaded by Bernard of Clairvaux with his tracts and sermons on the Song of Songs. The strongly erotic love songs about Christ composed by medical women mystics were also based on this symbolic interpretation. But all in all the central theme of mystical marriage was preserved (albeit in altered form) and given fresh life.

Leaving aside these two attempts at interpretation, modern research into the Song of Songs has reached conclusions which should be referred to at least briefly, because they shed light on the subject.[4] As individual songs were examined to see if they came from the ample store of folk-music, it was decided that the Song of Songs came for the most part from worldly sources. The frankly erotic choice of words and the richly allusive imagery in dialogue and description point directly to such a derivation. And it is consistent with the nature of genuine symbolism. Whoever takes too literally what is meant symbolically will miss the point. So it follows, as Hartmut Schmökel[5] in particular finds, that the symbolism of the Song of Songs is consistent with the earliest manifestations of *Hieros Gamos* between Tammuz and Ishtar, Baal and Astarte — even if individual questions by their nature remain open.

In summarizing his independent research Schmökel gives his opinion that *inter alia*:

The openly erotic language of the text in the mouth of a young girl, and especially the references to coupling with a lover, are unthinkable for the village sweetheart and bride of an Israelite of Palestine, but would accord fully with the manner and behaviour of Ishtar — the 'sacred model of the gods'. . . In many respects this description of bride and bridegroom hardly fits a rural couple of the Old Testament or an ancient Semitic peasant wedding. A bridegroom from the 'wilderness' or 'the mountain' would be meaningless and profane, but in the Tammuz mystery it could portray the underworld from which the dead return. The procession in 3:6 evokes Jehovah's appearing on Mount Sinai and goes back eventually to the Babylonian New Year festival procession. The searching and watchman passage of 3:1ff. and the lover in 8:5f. can be understood in terms of Ishtar's journey into Hell. . . The description of the beloved in 5:10ff. has in mind a cult statue of gold, ivory and marble. . . The praise of the beloved, 'therefore do the virgins love thee' 1:3, fits in with Tammuz 'darling of women' as in Ezekiel 8:14. The well-known naked dance of the bride in 7:1ff. is not of a village bride but is very possibly of the goddess of love or her representative in the orgiastic feast of Ishtar. The nuptials under fir and cedar of 1: 16-17 are no village-green wedding, but the bridal chamber of mystical marriage under another name. Accordingly in its origin the Song of Songs must have had to do with a cult liturgy which celebrated the holy marriage of two Palestinian deities, not inconsistent with the Sumerian-Babylonian pair, Ishtar and Tammuz.[6]

Thus the Song of Songs may be seen as a reworking of liturgies celebrated in the ancient East in connection with mystical marriage. But it does not appear to be a simple borrowing from Babylonian-Aryan models. As Hartmut Schmökel emphasizes:

It was no unfamiliar god who rose from the dead and wedded the goddess of love; it was a local Baal or even a Jehovah of popular religion venerated in a Canaanite form whose spring festival was celebrated; the name Tammuz which Ezekiel preferred (8:14) possibly had a foreign origin. . . but there was an Israelite Tammuz. . .

under which name his worship may have continued... and it was the lilies of Sharon and the camphor of Engedi which perfumed him; the pools of Heshbon, David's tower and the shining black coats of the goats of Gilead are familiar images in his songs.[7]

In short the Song of Songs is a 'thoroughly Israelite book' which praised mystical marriage, affirming a fruitful sensuality and at the same time poetically glorifying Jehovah's love for His beloved, the 'virgin Israel'.

Is the Song of Songs then only a literary work expressing a 2,500 year old tradition from a historical viewpoint? Surely not. In fact it is only now, when plausible arguments about the origin and meaning have been aired, that modern readers — of both sexes — can join in its experience at first hand. Instead of paying all their attention to literary-historical arguments readers can let the images work *on them*, listen to the song, and follow the rhythm of this hymn of praise. Direct communication becomes possible. Poetry becomes reality. They sense that the poetry of mystical marriage may become part of their *own* inner experience.

> Set me a seal upon thine heart
> As a seal upon thine arm
> For love is strong as death.

Appendix: Mandragora, The Fertility Plant

Before we pursue our subject in the New Testament we should refer in passing to a theme which appears occasionally in the Old Testament and is incorporated into ecclesiastical tradition by a remarkable number of Church fathers and mystics.[1]

Chapter 30 of Genesis tells the story of Reuben, son of Jacob, how he went into the field at harvest time and found the so-called *Duda'im* (mandragora; according to Buber, love berries), which he brought to his mother, Leah:

Then Rachel said to Leah, Give me, I pray thee, of thy son's mandrakes. And she said unto her, Is it a small matter that thou hast taken my husband? and wouldest thou take away my son's mandrakes also? And Rachel said, Therefore he shall lie with thee to night for thy son's mandrakes. And Jacob came out of the field in the evening, and Leah went out to meet him, and said, Thou must come in unto me; for surely I have hired thee with my son's mandrakes. And he lay with her that night. And God hearkened unto Leah, and she conceived, and bare Jacob the fifth son (Genesis 30:14-17)

The Song of Songs also recognizes its use as a fertility agent:
'The mandrakes give a smell, and at our gates are all manner
of pleasant fruits. . . (7:13). The Greek translation of the Old
Testament (the Septuagint) renders the Hebrew word as 'mandragora'. It is a plant that comes into full fruit in late spring,
and has a strong perfume. The fleshy root is striking, being
shaped like a human without a head. Roots and fruit have been
used for centuries in the concoction of medicines, especially
those supposed to have aphrodisiac or narcotic properties.
Mystical-symbolic significance followed on the heels of the
magical-pharmaceutical. Mandragora's use as a love potion was
bound to attract the disapproval of Bible commentators
whether in Genesis or the Song of Songs; and so mandragora
was regarded as a metaphor for a bride, and by extension
became a symbol of mystical marriage and eventually became
widely known throughout the Middle Ages. Even the scepti-
cal view of the Augustinian missionary Alcuin did not change
this romantic view. Alcuin, court theologian of Charlemagne,
suggested this allegory:

In its medicinal uses the mandragora is like the virtues of holy men.
The 'doors' on which it hangs are like the holy teachers of the
Church. It spreads its perfume at the door as holy men breathe out
the perfume of their virtue far and wide.

Hugo Rahner, who has researched many instances and interpretations of the drug, says that there are many similar examples.
Mandragora's change of meaning from a means of sexual magic
to a symbol of a mystical Christian bride became an accepted
fact wherever there was allegorical thinking about the loving
union of God and man, of Christ and the Church. Thus Hieronymus equates the hitherto childless Rachel with the Church,
buying Jacob's love with the sweet-smelling mandrake.

In the Trudbert Song of Songs, an old High German ver-
sion, Christ himself appears 'as the godly gardener who
descends into the darkness of the material world in order to
pluck the mandrake of the human race (which lets out a deathly
wail as it is picked) and, through the power of his incarnation,
bestow on it eternal flowering and fragrance.'[2]

Honorius Augustodunensis (c. 1080-c. 1156), who saw in the
Song of Songs a judgement-day drama in which four queens
approach Christ the bridegroom from the four cardinal points

of the heavens, announced the solemn coronation of the mandragora. Growing out of the earth without a head, it takes Christ as its head; in this way the New Testament apocalyptic meaning is fulfilled. Queen Mandragora is an 'eternal Israel' which (in contrast to a Christ-denying synagogue) is worthy of union with Christ. Honorius writes:

After the whole retinue of the Shulamite [i.e. the bride of the Song of Solomon] was received into the King's court for the royal wedding, behold from the north, with majestic pageantry, a new bride is led in to the bridegroom: namely, the headless mandrake. The bridegroom sets upon her a golden head, embellished with a crown, then she too is led to the wedding. When the Shulamite leaves the royal city she finds the mandrake, the royal maiden, headless again, lying in a field. Seized with pity, she returns to the King and beseeches him to accompany her and have mercy on the unhappy creature. So the King goes with the Shulamite to the field, finds the maid in her pitiable nakedness, lifts her up, clothes her, puts a golden head upon her and takes her into his bridal chamber... Now the bridegroom too puts on a golden head to show his divinity (which surpasses all others as gold surpasses all other metals). So she is crowned with glory and honour and he will marry her openly as part of his ceremonial. The headless mandrakes are thus the heathen, lacking Christ the head, and from whom their head, the Antichrist, has been struck off.[3]

In this way the love-awakening, soul-healing (and also sin-forgiving) plant becomes a symbol of the union of Christ with his Church — in other words with those who were formerly without a head, i.e. without Christ. Only through marriage with him will they become whole. It should be mentioned here that mandragora had a definite place in medieval herbal medicine. Reference should be made for example to the prescriptions of Hildegard von Bingen which specifically recommended mandragora when men or women 'are incontinent as a result of magical influence or natural disturbance.'[4]

3

Attitudes to Marriage in the New Testament

It may at first sight seem surprising to be looking for mystical marriage in the New Testament. Yet its symbolism and associated imagery and vocabulary occur there more than is generally recognized; and this is true of the whole Testament — the Gospels, the Epistles and the book of Revelation. It is clear that in pursuing this question we have to move away from Eastern models of *Hieros Gamos*, as had already happened in ancient Israel, where it was not a matter of orgiastic nuptials of the gods but where the Lord Jehovah himself looked favourably on the 'virgin Israel' and renewed their marriage bonds, despite her desertion and lack of faith.

In any case the metaphors of bride and bridegroom, of the great wedding feast and of the apocalyptic event of the 'marriage of the Lamb' (Revelation 19:7, 9) are to be found in the New Testament as part of the basic testimony taught in the parables. These images are closely related to spiritual union with Christ; a union full of joy. Paul speaks of 'being in Christ' and 'being members of his body' — a body of which Christ is the head — while according to John, among others, the allegory of the vine is used to show that only the branches 'that abide in' him can bear fruit. To be a part of Christ is to take part in life. To eat and drink with him is to have a foretaste, as it were, of communion with him 'in his Kingdom'. And just as the union of man and woman, bride and bridegroom 'as one flesh' is repeatedly stressed, so the symbol of marriage directs our attention to the last eschatological unity of the whole creation under God, in God — the goal of human longing.

The central message of the Gospels is the love of God for mankind — 'God so loved the world' (John 3:16) — and the love of human beings for God, which they show not least in love of their fellows. Walter Schubart goes so far as to say, 'No other religion sees the union between God and man in such a sensual light, and as a mutual bond of love. . . Christianity is a religion of rapturous salvation. It offers the widest scope for a redeeming love to be experienced in religious terms.'[1] But we should note that the full depths of the agape as the giving of selfless devotion is not yet given expression here. Nevertheless Schubart has drawn attention to the fact that physical love is not all that much of a stranger to the Christian message. And it is significant that not since Hosea and the Song of Songs have we met with such sensual language (and its attendant emotion), allowing us a singular opportunity to approach the mysterious boundaries of man's union with God.

Let us now turn to Jesus. The teacher and preacher Jesus of Nazareth enters the scene at a time which the people, subjugated by the occupying power of the Romans, had excited expectations of an apocalyptic event, as the impatience of the Zealots showed. Jesus disassociated himself from the aims of the dominant groups: the Pharisees, the Sadducees, the ascetic disciples of John the Baptist, and the strict 'Sons of Light', the Essenes, who went their own way, carefully preserving the purity of their sect so as to prepare 'the way in the desert' for the long-awaited Messiah. Referring to the Qumran texts (the Dead Sea Scrolls) which have been made more available in the last four decades, we find the symbol of the bridegroom, though he is still far off. The Essenes' message was of a great 'Not yet'. On the other hand the message of Jesus was that 'the hour cometh and now is' (John 4:23). For them there was expectation; but here was the beginning of fulfilment: the Kingdom of Heaven is (already) nigh! Taken literally, the theme of marriage has become current news.

The stranger calls himself the 'Son of Man', a name to be found in the prophetic book of Daniel (7:13). In the 'night visions' of the prophet he appears with the 'clouds of heaven'. He will be invested with the Kingdom, the power and the glory. Jesus submits to comparison with the Pharisees and John's disciples. In Mark (2:18f.) he is asked, 'Why do the disciples of John and of the Pharisees fast, but thy disciples fast not? And Jesus said unto them, Can the children of the bridechamber fast, while the bridegroom is with them? As long as they have the bridegroom with them, they cannot fast.'

In this way Jesus neatly described the situation. Jewish custom might prescribe fasting to prepare for the Sabbath or feast days or to express grief, but for Jesus and his followers a new era had begun. The time for mere waiting, mourning or even preparation is over. *Now* is the time for rejoicing; now is marriage, time for joy; the bridegroom is here, so celebrate with him. The days will come when the bridegroom shall be taken away for a time, but the presence of the Son of Man signals the start of the wedding celebrations. This is the mood that runs through the Gospels: marriage as a figure of speech for the new Being that Christ represents. 'Since fasting is a sign of turning back, the beginning of the wedding brings salvation and forgiveness. And as mankind need not make approaches to God but rather God approaches mankind, so fasting may cease and the disciples of Jesus may celebrate and rejoice in the gift of God's creation.'[2]

Even if Hosea and the author (or authors) of the Song of Songs had Jehovah's relation with Israel to celebrate as betrothal or indeed as an enjoyable 'love affair' (as Böhme later called it), nevertheless the 'new union' was in no way inferior to the old — on the contrary. In fact the twelfth-century Calabrian visionary, Abbot Gioacchino of Fiore, glorified the new kingdom of Son and Holy Ghost as against the old kingdom of Jehovah in ever new and stronger turns of phrase.[3] We may well infer that he implies a concept of mystical marriage when he speaks of a 'new union' or a 'New Testament'. Some Christian denominations, especially puritanical Nonconformists, have rejected the symbol of marriage along with idolatry, and one of them has declared real truth to lie with the old fasting religion. However, it is no accident that in the same passage that speaks of marriage and an end to fasting we find the expressions 'new wine' and 'new bottles':

And no man putteth new wine into old bottles; else the new wine doth burst the bottles, and the wine is spilled, and the bottles will be marred: but new wine must be put into new bottles (Mark 2:22).

Again in the course of Church history we shall come across what was (considered against the background of the religious situation in Palestine at the time) an enthusiastic, seemingly quite 'free-thinking' attitude. It was an attitude that broke down boundaries and frontiers whenever an over-restrictive legal framework hampered intellectual freedom and confined charisma 'to official channels'. In the context of the above quotation from St Mark's Gospel, 'new' means nothing less than the Kingdom of God born in Christ. It is no accident that, here and later, Jesus used wine in his parables. For in ancient Israel wine was *the* drink associated with weddings. And was not the house of Israel itself the vineyard of the Lord Jehovah (Isaiah 5:7)? At the same time wine is contrasted with the drink the Son of Man was to refuse — the water stored in jars and serving for purification, a rite belonging to the old order.

This brings us to the first miracle in the Gospel according to St John (2:1-11).[4] Is it by chance that the words *bridegroom* and *marriage* appear at the beginning of St Mark's Gospel, and the wedding in Cana in Galilee is the first of seven miracles performed by Christ in St John's Gospel? It is a wedding, therefore, which constitutes a prelude, as it were, to the impact of the newly-arrived Messiah. How naturally it is assumed that Jesus, his mother and his disciples should be invited to the wedding, and how curious that so little is said of the bridegroom and even less of the bride. There is a mystery pervading the event.

Hieronymus Bosch[5] sought to capture this sense of mystery in his painting, the *Marriage at Cana*. The bride and groom are indeed sitting in the centre of this Galilean village wedding, but the real action emanates from the man who sits inconspicuously at one side. A gentle gesture of blessing is hinted at; his presence is everything, the 'real presence' at that holy meal.

'Whatever *he* [my italic] saith unto you, do it.' These puzzling words came not from the bridal pair or from the 'master of ceremonies' but from 'the mother' of Jesus. Why exactly is the name 'Mary' avoided? Is there a similar mysterious link between 'him' and 'her' as between 'him' and his 'hour' which is not yet come, but which nevertheless does come unexpectedly to reveal the true nature of his glory [Greek: *doxa*] (John 2:11)?[6] This puzzling 'hour' connects the miracle at the wedding with the hour of his death. But nothing of this is visual, so there is nothing for Bosch to paint but the event from the outside. However, the eye of the believer sees more than what is there for the ordinary eye to see. Indeed it is this *eye of the believer* that is a mark of the true disciple. The chance wedding guest becomes the central figure. Only now does the true bridegroom come into view, as in the spirit of this Bible passage which immediately precedes the wedding: 'Ye shall see heaven open, and the angels of God ascending and descending upon the Son of Man' (John 1:51).

In other words, from now on any disciple of Christ to whom his full glory is revealed may perceive in an everyday Galilean village wedding a future with new qualities of life-giving power. From now on the vision (that is, of the believer) will be set

Figure 1: The *Marriage at Cana*, by Hieronymus Bosch. (Boymans Museum, Rotterdam. From Carl Linfert, *Hieronymus Bosch*, Phaidon, Cologne, 1959.)

free for the ultimate Holy Marriage. What happens in Cana
is not an end but literally a beginning — the beginning of the
miracles which Jesus was to perform. And this beginning goes
beyond what is portrayed now to the marriage of the future.
Here at the centre are man and wife, bride and bridegroom;
but in the sky above them is the conjunction of sun and moon;
in the Kingdom of the Spirit there is a higher order of marriage. And indeed is not this woman of the Apocalypse clothed
with the sun, and the moon under her feet (Revelation 12:1)
meant to symbolize the 'great miracle', the apotheosis of the
'miracle of Cana'? To go back again to the symbols used in
the marriage:

There is the symbol of water influenced by the moon, and the symbol of wine influenced by the sun. Sun and moon interact with one
another in the physical world, in the human world, in the Kingdom
of the Spirit and in the world of heavenly bodies. It is the same power
that flows between the sun and moon, Christ and Mary-Sophia, husband and wife, water and wine. Out of the combination of sun and
moon, male and female, will be created a radiant man-woman, a quin-
tessential whole human being, transfigured in body, mind and soul.[7]

So in a marriage ceremony the believer's attention must take
in different aspects. And because Christian belief is not directed
towards (impersonal) actions or reactions but towards Christ
alone, the belief has quite another dimension. It is very closely
linked with the miracle of Cana; for belief itself then creates
a subtle yet none the less real link: the believer is wedded to
Christ, and Christ to the believer. And this inner experience
of mystical marriage is related to the disciples' feelings when
they observed the external appearance of the wedding at Cana.
The evangelist points in this direction (John 2:11): 'This *beginning of miracles* did Jesus in Cana of Galilee, and manifested forth
his glory; and his disciples believed on him.'

   Again the question arises, what does this internal union consist of and what form does this internal marriage take, as it is
to be experienced again and again, for example, by male and
female mystic alike?

   The coming of the Messiah was held to imply a marriage.
This view, widely held in the Jewish community, was expressed
by John the Baptist when he first saw Christ. As a forerunner
he had to build a bridge between the old covenant and the new.
Mark's Gospel had already distinguished between Jesus and

John the Baptist, and St John's Gospel refines the distinction (3:28ff). First there is the clear statement: 'I am not the Christ, but that I am sent before him.' And then comes the remark: 'He that hath the bride is the bridegroom.'

John the Baptist therefore took the fact of a wedding for granted; it was indeed a new covenant. The betrothal of Jehovah and Israel had become part of history. John the Baptist was content to be 'the friend of the bridegroom' and undertake the role of marriage broker and 'go-between', in those days an essential function. By this time the bridegroom's voice is plainly to be heard, though John the Baptist would not live to see the promise fulfilled. Just as the dying Moses saw the Promised Land but was not allowed to set foot upon it, so John the Baptist foresaw the imminent marriage of bride and groom. And so the bridegroom's friend can say of him: 'This my joy therefore is fulfilled' (John 3:29). So as this key point was reached, of seeing the age-old phenomenon of the mystical marriage of the heavenly bridegroom in a Galilean village wedding, that is, of seeing it as a believer, it had to suffice for John the Baptist, the forerunner of the Messiah, simply to hear the bridegroom's voice. And we should note yet another instance from these stories about John the Baptist: we should see him for the moment as shown by the painter Grünewald, with an oversized finger pointing as he continues, 'He must increase but I must decrease.' The significance of these words is their meaning in the language of astrology.[8] They refer to the waning of the moon and the rising of the sun. However, this is not to be thought of as a cyclical exchange between moon and sun through the course of the year. The movement the Baptist describes is not reversible, though the sun loses strength again and the moon is renewed. The spirit which John the Baptist represents will not gather renewed strength at the expense of the Christ-sun. This is one of the fundamental differences between Christ's advent in 'the fullness of time' (Galatians 4:4) and the 'annually recurring' marriage of the pagan gods, which was to ensure the fertility of the earth. Wilhelm Stählin comments on this:

The image of the wedding and the friend of the bridegroom removes Christ's background from the world of natural scenes and events and sets it in the personal domain. Thus the word of Christ can be identified with an increase in personal spirituality. Spirituality consists of a diminution of the old Adam in us and growth of the Christ within us.

Spirituality is a weakening of purely natural instincts.[9] These, we should add, are not entirely superseded or 'destroyed'. God's love for man does not make the procreative instinct and sex superfluous or entirely to be condemned; agape deepens and complements them. The theological analysis then, aiming at 'perfection', can (if enriched by a psychoanalytic interpretation) be seen as concerned with 'completing' the development of man's soul. And marriage, mystical marriage especially, is the embodiment and archetype of this completion of the human being who, feeling 'half-a-person', seeks out his or her 'better half'!

The eschatological trend, directed towards the future of Christ, is insisted on in St Matthew's Gospel, where Jesus, drawing near his 'hour', puts before his disciples an image of his impending Passion and thereby sharpens their inner perception. He tells them the famous parable of the ten wise and ten foolish virgins, told to attend the bridegroom's wedding with lamps burning brightly, that is to say well-prepared and in the clear light of awareness:

Then shall the kingdom of heaven be likened unto ten virgins, which took their lamps, and went forth to meet the bridegroom (Matthew 25:1).

The bridegroom is once again the Son of Man. This time waiting for the wedding is complicated by the uncertainty of the hour when the bridegroom will call his guests to the wedding feast: 'And at midnight . . . the bridegroom cometh' (Matthew 25:6). There is a shadow cast over this parable reflected in the fact that Christendom, after Easter and Whitsuntide, counts so earnestly on the certain coming of Christ, for in effect the 'bridegroom is missing'. The time of his coming and indeed the time of the wedding itself (though definite for each individual) is unknown. Therefore it is vital to be prepared, to have enough oil so that the lamp can overcome the dark night when eyelids hang heavy with sleep. We are not told what the wise virgins' oil represented. In the New Testament's equivalent to the Song of Songs (1 Corinthians) it is not a question of bridesmaids and wedding but rather of what 'abides', what has the spiritual power to illuminate the darkness: 'And now abideth faith, hope, charity [love], these three; but the greatest of these is charity [love].'

Is the whole New Testament suffused with the spirit of marriage? Paul is no stranger to this theme. On the contrary, the apostle was very aware that he was entering an area of mystery. Straightaway he behaves like a best man, just as John the Baptist had understood the role he should play. So Paul writes without hesitation to the Corinthians that his task is to present the congregation 'as a chaste virgin to Christ' (2 Corinthians 11:2). The people's apostle is cast in the role of a marriage broker! That this 'presentation to Christ' implies a picture, a form of perfect beauty, is borne out in Paul's epistle to the Colossians, which describes his apostolic task as being to 'present every man perfect in Jesus Christ' (Colossians 1:28).[10] The epistle to the Ephesians continues the symbolic language of marriage literally, when Paul describes the bridegroom himself performing the function of best man, 'that he might present it *to himself* a glorious church' (Ephesians 5:27). That is to say that mystical marriage cannot be arranged as we may wish. The decisive action comes not from mankind but from Christ. He is not only the bridegroom; he also leads us into the communion, which he offers as salvation and life. He is not only the embodiment of a divided mankind — divided from God, divided from other humans, divided from its own self — as best man he is also in command of all cosmic power.

It is remarkable how the epistle to the Ephesians presents two opposing material and spiritual aspects of the matter and then reconciles them: one passage stresses the physical, another the spiritual — on the one hand sexual union between husband and wife, on the other spiritual union between Christ and his Church (*ecclesia*). The views expressed are difficult to accept today, representing as they do a decidedly patriarchal order, in which the husband is head of the household and the wife is his inferior (Ephesians 5:22ff.). Much closer to us is the apostle's next remark when he particularly enjoins the husband to love his wife with all his heart, 'even as Christ also loved the church and gave himself for it' (Ephesians 5:25), and then says, 'he might sanctify and cleanse it with the washing of water by the word'. The Catholic theologian and mystic Odo Casel regards this baptism of water as nothing less than 'the bridal bath of the church'. Franz Mussner, in his study of the Epistle to the Ephesians, comes to this conclusion:

Today once we see the relationship of Christ with the church as an image of marriage, we cannot deny that in Ephesians 5:26, 27 the image of baptism as the bridal bath of the church is deliberate. At the same time it is essential to understand it correctly: its setting is in a religious, moral context.[11]

The ritual bridal bath can only follow marriage. Paul, who was celibate, referred back to the Old Testament (Genesis 2:24) when in Ephesians 5:31 he wrote: 'For this cause shall a man leave his father and mother, and shall be joined unto his wife: and they two shall be one flesh.' Then comes the key passage: 'This is a great mystery [*mysterion*]: but I speak concerning Christ and the church.' The union of man and wife follows this union with Christ, and indeed it is the act of love which is its special quality. It is more than a partnership, more than a civil contract, it is a mystery, the mystery of the male-female unit, which as husband-and-wife is not 'one' unless he or she experiences union both outwardly and *within* him- or herself.

This is admittedly only *one* aspect of the 'blessed longing' which has always inspired mankind from time immemorial. Alongside the individual, the interpersonal and the cosmic aspects, one has to keep in mind (at the very highest level) the eschatological or apocalyptic aspect. The Revelation of St John the Divine refers to it. The great apocalyptic beatitudes include this saying: 'Blessed are they which are called unto the marriage supper of the Lamb' (Revelation 19:9). Then there is the great vision we have already mentioned briefly (Revelation 12:1-6): 'And there appeared a great wonder in heaven: a woman clothed with the sun, and the moon under her feet.' This female figure brings forth 'a man child'. It seems the prophet wants to say that with this birth a new age has come, namely that of 'God the Ruler' and the Kingdom of Heaven. Ernst Lohmeyer observes that this mystical theme which runs through religious history is not isolated in this passage, but continues with further development right to the end of Revelation. 'It is typical of it that the boy, growing up to manhood, seizes power and crowns it through *Hieros Gamos* with a goddess; so Virgil declared in the Fourth Eclogue...'[12] In Virgil's great secular nativity poem from the first century BC, that is 150 years earlier than Revelation, there are verses which foretell the birth of a boy and allude finally to his marriage:

Now is come the last age of the song of the Sybil; the great line of the centuries begins anew. Now the Virgin returns, the reign of Saturn returns; now a new generation descends from heaven on high... Do thou smile on the birth of the child, under whom the iron brood shall first cease, and a golden race spring up throughout the world... Begin, baby boy, to know thy mother with a smile — to thy mother ten months have brought the weariness of travail. Begin, baby boy! Him on whom his parents have not smiled, no god honours with his table, no goddess with her bed![13]

Christianity obviously distinguishes between the first advent of Christ the Messiah and the second, the true coming of Christ on the Day of Judgment.

In Revelation 19, a completely new hymn rings out:

And I heard as it were the voice of a great multitude, and as the voice of many waters, and as the voice of mighty thunderings, saying, Alleluia: for the Lord God omnipotent reigneth. Let us be glad and rejoice, and give honour to him: for the marriage of the Lamb is come, and his wife hath made herself ready. And to her was granted that she should be arrayed in fine linen, clean and white (Revelation 19:6-8).

Such a hymn about the close fellowship of Christ and his Church is more than a theological statement. It is intended to bring about an inner experience in those who receive the revelation. We have seen the image of divine marriage already illustrated in the Old Testament, for example when Jehovah's love for Israel is described in Hosea (2:19-20):

And I will betroth thee unto me for ever; yea, I will betroth thee unto me in righteousness, and in judgment, and in lovingkindness, and in mercies. I will even betroth thee unto me in faithfulness: and thou shalt know the Lord.

This mystical marriage then aims also at a deeper understanding of God. There is no lack of erotic language in the stories. Ezekiel (16:7-8), for example, draws a picture of Jehovah approaching the virgin Israel in these words:

And thou hast increased and waxen great, and thou art come to excellent ornaments: thy breasts are fashioned, and thine hair is grown, whereas thou wast naked and bare. Now when I passed by thee, and looked upon thee, behold, thy time was the time of love; and I spread my skirt over thee, and covered thy nakedness: yea, I sware unto thee, and entered into a covenant with thee, saith the Lord God, and thou becamest mine.

But this biblical picture of mystical marriage still lacks the final eschatological dimension. This begins to appear only in

Figure 2: The new Jerusalem 'prepared as a bride adorned for her husband' (Rev. 21.2), presented as the union of the Holy City with Christ the bridegroom. ('The Cloisters Apocalypse', fol. 36, New York, Metropolitan Museum of Art. From Edward F. Edinger, *The Anatomy of the Psyche*, La Salle, Illinois, 1986.)

the New Testament when the Son of Man himself steps forward, first as suitor then as the bridegroom. But it becomes clear only in Revelation, how all these images of betrothal and marriage are to be seen in relation to this ultimate horizon. The individual and socio-theological dimensions here broaden out to encompass the cosmic and universal: 'And I, John saw the holy city, new Jerusalem, coming down from God out of heaven, prepared as a bride adorned for her husband (Revelation 21:2).[14]

With a book such as Revelation we have to be constantly asked what particular imaginative elements and figures mean. Otherwise we might as well resign ourselves (as Luther did) to its remaining a closed book to us. Yet however striking the image of the bride of the Lamb may be in a context of eschatological drama, one theological commentator makes further use of allegorial language when he says: 'When it has come to perfection, the church enters into the eschatological Kingdom of God and in a future Holy City becomes a blessed congregation, a new creation, the fulfilment of all God's plans for the world and its redemption.[15] We should not overlook the fact that the last book of the Bible was written at a time of persecution of Christians (under the Emperor Domitian). So what we have is a document from a martyred church. But such contemporary references are overlaid with more universal symbols such as evil in the form of a dragon which threatens a pregnant woman (Revelation 12) or the 'Whore of Babylon' whom one can recognize as representing the towers of that evil city. Each is a form of human hubris which heaven will overcome, a base edifice to be razed to the ground as Jerusalem itself comes down as a bride from heaven, that is, from God, to meet the expectant world.

The theme of mystical marriage seems to have been replaced by that of the Holy City. Once we are shown the numbers and dimensions of the Heavenly Jerusalem, they speak an unmistakably symbolic language which points to completeness, integrity and perfection. The cosmic number twelve dominates, as a threefold four: the walls have twelve gateways watched over by twelve angels, on the gates are the names of the twelve tribes of the Old Testament covenant, illumined by twelve precious stones and twelve pearls. The prophet also describes how an angel with a golden reed measures the walls of the four-cornered city and finds that it is 'the measure of man'. The 'new creation which the Eternal City represents' is 'as profoundly humanistic as it is spiritual'.[16] Indeed it is a new humanity which 'sets the pattern' here. A new humanity represented by twelve-times-twelve a thousandfold — 144,000. Is this not a mystical number to express the union of the whole world with Christ? Corresponding numbers hold true for the Heavenly City which is the same in length, breadth and height and therefore forms a single, perfect cube.

This harmony of the dimensions of space corresponds to a 'mystical marriage' of light. The alternation of night and day is absorbed into a new quality of light: 'And the city had no need of the sun, neither of the moon, to shine in it: for the glory of God did lighten it, and the Lamb is the light thereof.' Sun and moon, the cosmic male and the cosmic female, have become one; the new earth has become one with the sun. Even so the metaphors, the symbols, the parables and signs of belief are hardly enough to explain completely the great mystery of becoming whole. . .

In spite of this (indeed because of it) the symbol of mystical marriage has gone on exercising a power of fascination — whether with devout medieval mystics, as in Jan van Ruysbroeck's fourteenth-century meditation, *The Spiritual Espousals*; or with the imaginary Christian Rosenkreutz and his Rosicrucian brethren who invented 'Chemical Marriage'. It was not enough to experience mystical marriage deep within the soul, but parts of the material world had to be incorporated 'chemically' into this great event of integration. Mankind's longing is great: it reaches out into popular fairy tales which often have their climax in the mystery of inner marriage. 'We can catch fleeting glimpses of the apocalyptic vision of Christ running through fairy tales in poetic form.'[17]

4

Gnostic Mysteries

'Who were we? What have we developed into? Where did we come from? What is this world into which we have been pitched? Where are we rushing to? From what have we been set free? What is birth? What is rebirth?'[1]

These basic questions touch upon problems fundamental for every human being. But the way in which they are formulated draws attention to a particular answer — that found in the concept of gnosis, the basis of the gnosticism of the early Christians. And because what is involved here is a question of unification (especially reunification of what has been separated) we would expect the gnostic movement of early Christendom to have something to say on the subject.

First let us look briefly at the background. The Greek word *gnosis* means knowledge. Like *pistis*, faith, it is one of the key words of the New Testament. This knowledge, however, is of a particular kind. It is not to be confused with a philosophical or rational approach. Gnosticism aims at establishing religious knowledge, and therefore 'claims no rational foundation. Gnosis is not a philosophy.'[2] Gnostic knowledge began as a spontaneous, inner consciousness: I realize that the world I live in is not my true home, the body I inhabit, like the material world itself, is totally alien. The gnostic must then further reflect: until the light of gnosis shines within me I have not found my real self, I am estranged from my true being. If my material body is a prison, where then do I come from? Where is my true home?

The gnostic's answer is that the true home of mankind is the brighter, higher, spiritual world. From there comes a call to awaken to true life. This call then arouses memory of a long-lost, forgotten world of heavenly light. A messenger of light from this other world calls the wanderer home and sets him on 'a hidden, holy path to gnosis'. This turning round and progress towards man's true home begins on earth through a life of ascetic renunciation, or (paradoxically) through an ethic of libertinism. Such permissiveness, advocated by some gnostic sects, allowed, or even enjoined, a dissolute life. Carnal pleasures and the urges of the flesh were to be indulged in without, however, equating them to man's whole nature, since they were traced to the Demiurge, an evil creator of the world. His sinister handiwork, the physical body, was to be despised. Of course real liberation, the salvation which gnosticism arrived at, occurred with death. Finally and supremely, it came with the end of the material world and all its powers and substance.

If man's existence was not real until 'after death', that is until he reached a primordial existence in communion with a transcendent God (as gnostic schools held in their many myths of redemption), then it followed that man's task was to overcome his divided condition and to return to a state of wholeness. Historically gnosticism can be described as a 'world religion'[3] which reached out far beyond Christianity. Looked at overall, it was a religion of redemption which gave central meaning to *mysterium coniunctionis*, divine betrothal, mystical marriage. Full participation in liberating gnosis would allow those to whom grace is promised to be united with the spirit of a higher world and by this means to realize their full identity. Some examples will illustrate this.

First there is plenty of evidence of pre-Christian gnostic mysteries. In them the human soul is seen as a bride who receives the divine seed of light through *Hieros Gamos*, so that she then gives birth to a new spiritual being (*anthropos pneumatikos*). Hence the prayer of a Hermetic mystic: 'Grow within me Lord Hermes, as children grow in their mothers' wombs!' And the classically-educated Jew, Philo of Alexandria, an older contemporary of Jesus, puts strong emphasis on the symbol of mystical marriage. In his work it acquires a twofold meaning: first as marriage between the godhead and someone embodying holy power; and second as union between God and the soul of man, involving a particular part or faculty, possibly virtue. In both cases on the godly side the bridegroom can be symbolized by the Word — *logos* — 'In the beginning. . . the word was God' (John 1:1):

Both cases can also be most easily explained by analogy with the mystical rites which symbolically or practically represented the inwardly experienced spiritual union of the priest with the godhead, prompted by enlightenment (*epoptie*). God was seen by Philo as father and husband of Wisdom, who received from Him the divine seed and gave birth to the world as an only beloved Son made visible in the flesh; whom also the Word covered like a garment and entered, so that he became one with the Word.[4]

As Philo once put it:

Now let all your righteous words of wisdom come down and join with me, let your seed flow into me; oh, pass not by a soul profound, fruitful and in the bloom of youth. Call her to your presence and your service, fulfil her and get her with child.[5]

We see that this gnostic writer sometimes used strongly erotic metaphorical language to support his central point. There is no doubt, however, that he is using a figure of speech that applies to himself and means an inspiration or a realization that will set him free. At the same time the distance of this passage from the only parable in the New Testament which alludes to mystical marriage is considerable.

Documentation of second-century gnosticism depends somewhat on St Irenaeus of Lyons, an opponent of so-called psuedo-gnosticism. He writes in great detail about the teaching of Valentinus, a leading gnostic of Egyptian origin, and apparently well-known. According to him, Valentinus' gnostic system was divided into a hierarchy of paired spiritual essences — the *aeons*. At their head was the Original Pair (or *syzygy*, union of opposites) called *Bythos* (Abyss) and *Sige* (Silence). From the union of these two, other pairs resulted, first *Nous* (Understanding) and *Alethia* (Truth), and so on until at the end, the thirtieth aeon was *Sophia* (Wisdom). She wished to understand God's unfathomable nature and fell headlong into the dark pit of the physical and material, where she lay in need of redemption through the 'Saviour' Jesus.

The many pairs of aeons in Valentinus' system indicate that the gnostic sees the ground prepared for mystical marriage in the divine, spirit world. Without going further into the dramatic but obscure fate of individual aeons it can be said that Jesus, as a gnostic saviour, is joined in mystical marriage with the 'Mother' (Achamoth — Wisdom). The gnostic is similarly redeemed and gains entry to the mystery as a spiritual being now 'saved from the material world'. His mystical marriage is celebrated with one of the angelic beings who accompany the gnostic saviour. The gnostic himself assumes the role of the bride, and as such can receive the 'seed of light', that is, knowledge of God, and can bring forth the new being which he will now become. Here one of Nietzsche's pithy aphorisms is relevant: 'You will become who you are.'

Irenaeus reports how certain followers of Valentinus clothed gnostic knowledge and its process of salvation in the ceremonial of a cult. It involved mystical activity which has also been hinted at by other writers on the subject. The ceremonies, described only in the vaguest terms, were carried on in a so-called 'bridal chamber'. In its innermost sense this bridal chamber is the spiritual world (the pleroma, that is, the fulfilment of the aeons) towards which the wandering Earth-bound soul consciously strives — a place with no earthly dimensions. Irenaeus writes:

Some of them [i.e. Valentinus' followers] prepare a bridal chamber and an initiation in the prescribed form for those who are to be accepted into the mystery. This initiation they call 'the marriage of true souls' [pneumatic marriage] in imitation of the higher syzygies [i.e. the aeons arranged in pairs].[6]

The ecclesiastical opponents of gnosticism had to protest repeatedly at the licentiousness of many exponents of pseudo-gnosticism and charged their cults with sexual excess, but the rite of the bridal chamber may nevertheless have been kept free of all this. Earthly marriage may have been contrasted with heavenly marriage, but the latter was 'immaculate', just as mystical marriage:

Its purpose was obviously to look ahead and give sacramental sanction to the eschatological union with the pleroma which would be put forward as the bridal chamber. But this would not be by a sexual act or the not-uncommon kissing ceremony... Anything like that would conflict with the 'holy' nature of such a marriage.[7]

It seems likely that the rite of the bridal chamber was celebrated as a kind of sacrament of death, with anointing and incantation, and indeed, as the 'Holy of Holies', this would have had more meaning than any other form of service. In the 'Wedding Song' of the apocryphal Gospel of St Thomas, probably from Syrian sources, we can see with what devoted images this gnostic spiritual marriage is described. Thomas, who is presented here as the twin of Jesus, gives us the following song:

The damsel is the daughter of light, in whom consisteth and dwelleth the proud brightness of kings and the sight of her is delightful, she shineth with beauty and cheer. . . Her chamber is bright with light, and breatheth forth the odour of balsam and all spices, and giveth out a sweet smell of myrrh and Indian leaf, and within are myrtles strewn on the floor, and all manner of odorous flowers, and the door-posts are adorned with reeds. And surrounding her, her groomsmen keep her, the number of whom is seven, whom she herself hath chosen. And her bridesmaids are seven, and they dance before her. And twelve in number are they that serve before her and are subject unto her, which have their aim and their look toward the bridegroom, that by the sight of him they may be enlightened; and for ever shall they be with her in that eternal joy, and shall be at that marriage whereto the princes are gathered together, and shall attend at that banquet whereof the eternal ones are accounted worthy. . . and have drunk of the wine that giveth them neither thirst nor desire. And they have glorified and praised with the living spirit, the Father of truth and the Mother of wisdom.[8]

This and similar passages give us something of the mood of joyful anticipation, the sure hope in which the gnostic joins the crowd for a great wedding party, and not merely as a guest. For just as the heavenly 'Mother' Wisdom (Achamoth — Sophia) finds her saviour and redeemer from out of the stifling bonds of ignorance into which she had fallen, so the gnostic's soul draws close to the angel, as a bride to her bridegroom. Through union with the angel the soul will be lifted into a higher world, its true home. Mystical marriage is the image of this spiritual event:

In the sacrament of the consecrated bridal chamber, celestial union can be anticipated, even on Earth, and its ecstatic delight experienced: 'We must become at one with ourselves. First take grace through and from me. Adorn yourself as a bride who looks forward to her groom, so that I may be you and you me. In your bridal chamber accept the seed of light. . .'[9]

Mystical marriage, which at one time in the Middle East served as the foremost guarantee of the fertility of mankind, of his animals and of the Earth itself, has (in early Christian gnosticism) become linked closely with religious experience and salvation within the gnostic community (*ecclesia*). We cannot overlook, however, the difference between the exclusive characteristics of the early Gnostic 'community' and the all-embracing brotherhood of the New Testament shown by those invited to the wedding feast of the Lamb. For a long time there were doubts as to whether the reports on gnosticism, which came almost exclusively from religious opponents, did actually correspond to the facts. That is until positive proof came from a chance discovery. This proof came from an extensive find of manuscripts near Nag-Hammadi in upper Egypt in 1945-6. This sensational discovery consisted of a small but impressive library of original gnostic writings. It must be referred to here because these texts, going back to the second century, deal (in their preamble) with the ceremony of the bridal chamber. We find this in the so-called Acts of Philip and in a small work, *The Exegesis of the Soul.* According to the Acts of Philip the future salvation of mankind depends on carrying out the sacrament of the bridal chamber. By this means a way is made for the soul to rise into the upper bridal chamber. For, he goes on to say, 'Those who have received the perfect light cannot be seen or touched by [hostile] supernatural powers. And it is in the "mystery" and the "union" that one will receive this light.' Then further:

If one becomes as a child of the bridal chamber, one will receive the light. If one does not receive it when one is here [i.e. in this world] one will not be able to receive it in the other world. [i.e. in the world of light, of the pleroma] either. Whoever receives this light (in the bridal chamber) will (when he ascends to heaven) be neither seen nor held back.[10]

One of the fears that haunted the gnostic, and which he sought to overcome, was the possibility that hostile supernatural powers could hinder his ascent through the seven planetary spheres. In order to reach the upper bridal chamber he equipped himself with powerful secret passwords and with 'magic signs on his hands'. It was important for the gnostic of the Acts of Philip, as for the very similar followers of Valentinus, to include the gnostic symbols of wisdom in the practice of their cults. As the Acts show, a clear distinction was made between the symbol and real spiritual truth. The gnostic was convinced that what was enacted in the form of metaphorical imagery corresponded with what really happened in the higher world. In other words the rite of the bridal chamber in factual terms corresponded to a spiritual reality of mystical marriage in the world of the spirit. For as the gnostic evangelist reflects:

Truth came not naked into the world; rather it came clothed in symbols (*typos*) and images. The world cannot receive it otherwise. There is (for example) a real rebirth and one that is symbolic (a mirror image of the other). Truly the world must be born again through the image. The image must be redeemed through the image itself. The bridegroom and the image must arrive at the truth through the image and be made whole again... The Lord brought everything into one mystery: one baptism, one anointing, one Eucharist, one redemption, one bridal chamber...[11]

And just because all efforts failed to ensure that gnostic marriage was of a pure, spiritual nature, free from any scandalous practices, so the true character of the rites of the bridal chamber had to be constantly emphasized. So we read in the *Exegesis of the Soul*, one of the texts found at Nag-Hammadi with the Acts of Philip:

Now, according to the Father's will the bridegroom comes down to her (the bride [i.e. the gnostic]) in the bridal chamber made ready, the bridal chamber adorned by his presence alone. For this marriage is no carnal marriage, in which they seek to enjoy the pleasure of sexual union. They cast the torment of lust behind them like a burden and serve one another. In truth this is marriage of another kind and when they consummate this union they will become one single life.[12]

Understood in this way, the redeeming gnosis serves to overcome separation between man and God; between the soul of mankind as the bride and Christ, the bridegroom. Union with the bridegroom guarantees 'wholeness of life' in the body of Christ, in the sense of St John's Gospel. The symbolism of *Hieros Gamos* allows the gnostic to visualize this final eschatological end, and to examine it already on Earth, since Jesus made the way clear for gnosticism by his descent from Heaven.

In studying the human side of gnosticism, it is significant that the soul is cast in a female role. (Gnosticism is not alone in this.) The soul receives what is given to it from above, nothing less than the sperm of God, the seed of light. There is no question of self-redemption. 'This concept of the femininity of the soul finds its most important development in the holiness of the mystery, in the Gnostic teaching about vice and virtue... and finally in their teaching about grace.'[13]

When we consider that this early Christian gnostic mystery was almost completely eradicated by the 'orthodox' Church, and its rich literature, partly revealed, partly secret, was destroyed,[14] the question arises — within the limits of our subject — of how gnostic thought could possibly have been handed down to later times. In subsequent history there is little to give a picture of the tradition by which the symbol of mystical marriage has come down to us. So we shall concentrate more on other important phenomena through which the basic idea of this *mysterium coniunctionis* has repeatedly reappeared in new guises.

5

Conjugal Kabbalistic Mysteries

As the union of opposites is a central theme in the general history of religion, so mystical marriage, *Hieros Gamos*, is an important theme in the Kabbala, the Jewish mystery. It is described in this way in the fundamental kabbalistic text, the *Sefer ha-Zohar* or Book of Splendour:

When they (male and female) join together they appear as one flesh. From this we learn that the male alone appears as only part of a body: and so likewise does the female. But when they are joined together they appear as one body.

And further:

The young woman was united with the king. From this developed one flesh. From this arises the blessedness of these days. Thus we know that male or female alone are only part of a body. No blessing favours a thing that is blemished and incomplete, but falls only on that which is complete and not divided. For divided things cannot survive in the long run, and cannot be blessed.[1]

It is worth noting that these significant passages about the mystery of union are presented as a monologue by the dying Simeon ber Yohai, a great Talmudic authority and at one time reputed to be the author of this basic kabbalistic text. Thus death (which Dietrich Bonhoeffer, facing his own end, proclaimed to be 'the highest celebration on the way to eternal freedom') is closely associated with our human theme — marriage and death. And at the place designated for burial, the *Sefer ha-Zohar* continues:

When the coffin was carried out, it was lifted in the air and a fire burned before it. And they heard a voice saying, 'Arise and come, gather together for the wedding of Rabbi Simeon! Peace is here, you may rest secure in your villages.' When the coffin was brought into the vault they heard a voice therein 'that is he who shook the earth and made kingdoms tremble. What freedom has been won today through thee, Rabbi Simeon ber Yohai, in which daily our Lord takes pride? Happy his lot on high as upon earth below! What treasures are in store for him on high!'[2]

Let us look at some basic ideas which are set out in the so-called Sefirot tree of the Kabbalists.[3] The ten Sefirot, or reflected glories, can be understood on one hand as emanations of a hidden God (En Sof — the Infinite) who emerges from the darkness and acts wisely, with love and anger, with gracious beneficence and punitive judgement, and makes His presence (Schechina) felt by all creation. Also, and at the same time, the Sefirot tree represents an ontological man, i.e. presenting the perfectly fulfilled, eternal characteristics of mankind. In other words the ways in which God appears and the dynamic that the mysterious basis of His existence creates, correspond — *sub specie aeternitatis* — with humanity.

Setting out the tree graphically, the Kabbalists depict a ten-part structure in which individual branches or powers (reflected splendours) are related organically to one another. On this 'tree' the Kabbalist distinguishes not only a higher trinity represented by the Supreme Crown (Keter'elyon), Wisdom (Halhma) and Intelligence (Bina) but also — setting aside Malkhut/Schechina (Kingdom) — an intermediate and a lower trinity. He identifies right, centre and left classes of potential power. Seen in this way the system provides manifold means of interaction and polarities, which all work towards unity.

It is the tenth Sefira (Malkhut, Kingdom) which especially denotes the presence (Schechina) of God. It is an embodiment of the descent from heaven to earth of the One. It is His dwelling and His presence. But at the same time it represents the mystical body of the Knesset, that is, of the people of Israel. It bestows His love (Hesed) on the devout in their life and work. And in so far as it does this, it enters into direct union with the higher and the highest powers or the most secret essence of the godhead.

Here too this central spiritual experience is expressed in the language of love and in sexual symbolism. As we find throughout esoteric and mystical religious history, this means of expression like no other enables a deeply stirring experience to transcend the individual. And just as a person at the climax of a love affair surpasses him or herself ('in a flash' the mystic would say) so holy marriage, with its mystical attributes, an embodiment of a super-individualistic life-to-come. What is involved here is communion with the substance of an upper world. Faced with this experience, the human being can no longer remain what he was. He must become the person he should be. He is swept, as by a flood, into a new state of being. Whoever goes through such a peak of emotion knows that even the language of love and sex is not enough to capture its essence. Even this symbolic language must in the end be abandoned. It must be relinquished for a subjective non-physical experience. This is essential if one is to pass through the tem-

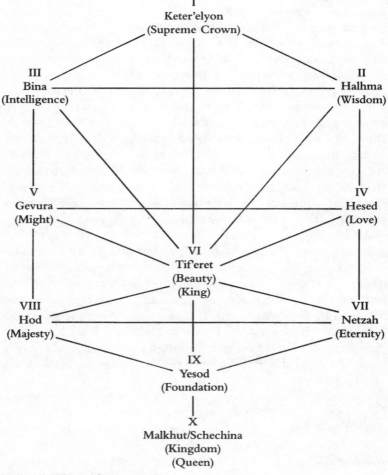

Figure 3: The Sefirot tree.

porary phase of ephemeral symbolism, above all if one is to avoid falling by simple misunderstanding into materialistic involvement or gross sexuality.

The secret of tension between opposites, and their unification, is indicated in several ways by the Sefirot tree. For one thing the right and left sides represent opposing poles. The right-hand side manifests the positive, love and masculinity, while the left-hand, the feminine side, manifests judgement, justice and the wrath of God. The central column performs a harmonizing, balancing function and therefore mediates between the two opposing principles. One need not point out that in assigning the male to the positive and the female to the negative principle there is no implication of greater or lesser value. Rather what is clear is that right and left, male and female, are always related to one another. It is only when one of them, for instance the negative principle, breaks away from the association, that destructive evil originates.

Another manifestation of the tension between opposites and their union in the Sefirot tree is in Tif'eret (Beauty) and Malkhut (Kingdom), which as King and Queen, or married woman, symbolize the male and female aspects of God. This also represents a holy union between God and his Schechina, representing the people of Israel. She is the bride of a heavenly bridegroom. Here the *Sefer ha-Zohar* speaks directly of mystical marriage (*Hieros Gamos* or [in Hebrew] *Siwwuga Kadisha*).

A further example of tension arises from the opposition of the ninth and tenth Sefirot, i.e. between on the one hand Yesod, also called Joseph the Just (into which all the higher Sefirot flow and which, in the human aspect of the tree, corresponds to an archetypal phallus) and on the other hand the married woman, Malkhut ('Kingdom'), or God's Schechina or living presence. Gershom Scholem explains these relationships thus:

The marriage of a holy king and queen is shown in a more general way through the union of Tif'eret and Malkhut, while the union of Yesod and Malkhut represents the narrower pattern of basic sexual union in the animal kingdom, without reference to wider aspects. When it occurs within the limits of sacred ordinances, the holiness of begetting as a genuine mystery is made plain in the *Sefer ha-Zohar* in repeated references to *Hieros Gamos* within the pattern of the Sefirot. Only when the prescribed limits are abandoned does sex become unholy, in which case it is seen as not just profane, but as devilish and depraved.[4]

This serves to remove any misunderstanding that may have arisen in previous paragraphs. There was no intention of sexualizing what was religious, particularly what was mystical. It was rather to *make holy what was physically sexual* in human experience. For devout Jews, for kabbalistic, especially Sephardic, mystics following Baal-Schem-Tow,[5] holiness dwelt essentially in material, bodily things. Consequently even strict Jewish ascetics, such as Simeon ber Yohai, abjured celibacy, for: 'when a man is alone without a wife there is no joy in his life.' But joy is the living expression of an inner relationship with God.[6] So it is not by chance that the *Sefer ha-Zohar* begins with an allegory that relates to the secret of mystical union, that of 'a rose between two thorns', and that the original author of kabbalistic wisdom should end his life with a didactic speech about the marriage of king and matron. By this means we have seen something of how the intense tension of opposites, of the opposing symbols of death and life, and in particular of love, is expressed. Above all, the Sefirot, Hesed and Gevura (or Din) correspond to the flowing waters of love and grace, and to the dark fire of strict justice, while Netzah and Hod indicate 'inseparable friends'. Halhma and Bina appear occasionally also personified to form a male-female pair of opposites, namely father and mother (especially world mother). So it was once said:

When the Ancient One — praised be his name — created form, he made everything in the form of male and female. Things cannot exist in other forms. That is why the very first development which began with Halhma was immediately male and female. That is to say Halhma as father and Bina as mother, from which everything else originated.[7]

The great theme of exile and the healing of alienation (by redemption) is also interwoven with mystical marriage. Thus for the Kabbalist the journey of the people of Israel home to the Promised Land had not yet been fully realized — it was not yet the moment when they would enter the land of their fathers and put an end to centuries of exile. We need to think of this in mystical-eschatological terms. The earthly return home is only an image, an allegory for the inner, holy process of redemption. It is the Schechina, God's presence, which wanders on earth and eventually returns home for union with God in the upper world. In the words of the *Sefer ha-Zohar*:

It is written: And there was evening and there was morning, *one* day. For there is no night without day and no day without night and they will be called one only because of their joining together in one unity. So will the Lord — praised be His name — be named as one together with the people of Israel [that is, the Schechina] but not while they are separated from one another. Because the people of Israel are now in exile they cannot be called one. When then will they be called one? That day when Israel is returned from exile and the people of Israel are returned to their place to unite there with the Lord—praise be to Him. That is what this verse means: Every day God will be one and His name will be one. But one without the other will not be called one.[8]

We have here a pietism that allows the mystery of union to be expressed on different levels: on the upper, divine level, indeed entering into the godhead itself; and on a lower, bodily level as between human beings. To dwell with God calls for renunciation of the corporeal, both in the history of peoples and its individual cases. However lower, bodily communion finds its true goal when the embrace of man and wife coincides with union on the divine level and as its equal. A puritanical dualism that tears the two apart and maintains they are incompatible with one another, is foreign to this religiosity. So the reflected glory of mystical marriage (*Siwwuga Kadisha*) covers the human union. Yet the natural act is not enough. Love and sex need, as it were, a link with the upper world. They must take place with true intention and due purpose (*Kawwana*) and consequently in sight of God's love and looking towards communion with Him. In short it is a question of fulfilling the requirements of mystical marriage.

Thus Gershom Scholem emphasizes:

The whole dynamic concept of God in the *Sefer ha-Zohar* is based on achieving a unity of divine life within *Hieros Gamos* and can in no way be separated from it. In fact the ever-present elaborate sexual symbolism and its interpretation so moved the author of the *Sefer ha-Zohar* with enthusiasm that it made difficulties for later theologians of the Kabbala ... while the higher Schechina is thought of as an eternal, indissoluble union with the upper Sophia, the Father, a union which remains wholly undisturbed by humans, the conjunction of king and queen is (in the present state of the world, that is, since the expulsion from Paradise) not a matter for God alone, but also one for humanity. Consequently mystical union is often quite intentionally subject to ritual. When man was banished from Paradise the 'lower mother', i.e. the Schechina, was also expelled. Indeed, as the famous passage (I.53b) has it in a daring exegesis, who expelled whom from Paradise is unclear — whether God mankind, or mankind God in the shape of the Schechina! Since then a central image in the *Sefer ha-Zohar* has been 'the exile of the Schechina' and that which should be the supporter and mediator of the combined powers of the earth is shown as separated from them. What is thus lacking must be made up by mankind.[9]

But how can this be done when mystical marriage takes place in the lower world as well as in the upper?

Also when the kabbalistic mystic penetrates to the heart of what he sees, it gives rise to a persistent longing to make the inner perceived experience outwardly manifest again. He wants to know it, so to speak, as one bewitched in love. He wants to feel the power of passion. Ritual, with the whole sequence of its sacred acts relating to the cult, is unique in enabling him to do this. Religious practices such as recitations, forms of prayer and accompanying gestures can be carried out and celebrated together by everyone within their respective traditions of piety. Such ritual can also be understood as the vehicle for a holy esoteric sacrament. For this there needs to be special esoteric knowledge which is obtained through initiation. What are generally profane human actions, such as eating, drinking and sexual union, become sacramental symbols which raise mankind above itself. 'This view of eating and sex is only peripheral in this context, for even if we are not talking about rabbinical Jewry, nevertheless in mystical thought generally these acts enter into the closest union with the realm of the sacramental.'[10] In trying to prove the whole Jewish ritual to be a kabbalistic mystery, rendering the transcendent visible (or making manifest the occult), the Jewish mystics have concentrated attention on their festival rites, especially on the celebration of the Sabbath. The presentation of mystical marriage acquires a central meaning both in the *Sefer ha-Zohar* and for later sympathetically-inclined Kabbalists, the more so as the Kabbalist sees in the two Sefirot Tif'eret (Beauty, King) and Malkhut (Kingdom, Schechina, Queen) the joining together of the male and female *in God*. Now the so-called Pentecost takes on a special meaning: it is celebrated fifty days after the Passion (Good Friday) and is a reminder of God's appearance on Mount Sinai. It is the ultimate contract between Jehovah and his people Israel; and for the mystic (for example Simeon ber Yohai, writing in the *Sefer ha-Zohar*) the compact is plainly holy marriage. The annual recurrence of Pentecost must therefore be suitably celebrated. The night before the festival its mystical meaning has to be remembered:

For this is the night when the bride prepares for her marriage with her husband, so it was deemed proper that everyone in the bride's household, i.e. the mystics and those well versed in the Torah, should keep her company and share with her a holy ritual of preparation for the wedding. It is the mystics who dress the Schechina in the correct finery which she will wear next morning under the marriage canopy.[11]

How else could preparation be made for marriage, other than by reciting the Torah, since it contains the core of divine wisdom, making up (with its store of hymns and prayers) twenty-four books of writing requiring special devotion (*Kawwana*)? The expert Kabbalist, who knows the mysteries since he knows the spiritual meaning of the scripture, therefore takes on the role of a father of the bride to the Schechina, the divine glory, which is ready to approach mankind, and will in its turn go to meet the bridegroom.

Gershom Scholem tells us how, from the beginning of the sixteenth century, the *Sefer ha-Zohar's* account of this marriage festival became the basis of an established ritual.

The night before the mystical marriage would be spent in vigil and in listening to agreed passages from the Scriptures, from the books of the Mishna, and also from those parts of the *Sefer ha-Zohar* itself pertaining to the festival. These would be recited, accompanied by songs. This ritual was extraordinarily popular and is widely practised even today. Indeed the image of a wedding would be maintained, in that the next day when the Torah was raised aloft in the synagogue and before the reading of the Ten Commandments, a formal Kabbalistic marriage contract between the 'bridegroom God' and the 'bride Israel' would be read out in many places.[12]

If this bond of communication with God is everlasting, then in the eyes of the Kabbalists the Jewish calendar is a perpetual reminder of what happened 3,000 years ago. That applies no less to the weekly Sabbath which starts on Friday evening, when the light of the upper world pleasantly brings to a close six weekdays in the earthly world. The Sabbath, which according to Scholem is a day celebrated in the Kabbala, is also a 'time of marriage'.* So individual teachers of the Talmud at one time

---

*Translator's note: the constituent parts of the German word *Hochzeit* (i.e. wedding or marriage) mean high, or holy, time.

took care, at evening prayers, to wrap themselves in a cloak and to call out, 'Come, let us go to meet the Queen Sabbath!' or they would call, 'Come, O bride, come O bride!' and in one of the kabbalistic hymns from the school of Moses Cordovero it says:

> Go, my beloved, to meet the bride
> Let us welcome the countenance of the Sabbath!

There, no doubt, speaks the strong, enthusiastic Messianic hope of ancient as well as of modern Israel. It is, however, also an expression of the happy embrace of man and wife. When, as was traditional, the Torah scholar took care to choose Friday night for union with his wife, the reason was that it was also on the night of the Sabbath that the divine King was joined with his Sabbath bride in mystical marriage. From this mystical union will spring the souls of the righteous, those who will form the foundation of the Kingdom of God. The earthly union of man and wife is the carnal counterpart of heavenly marriage. Thus this intercourse within marriage was valued as a mystery which had to be protected with the utmost reverence 'as the greatest of secrets'!

Gershom Scholem now gives us the following description of the kabbalistic Sabbath ritual:

Well before the Sabbath, at the time of evening prayers, the Kabbalists in the city of Zafat (the great traditional centre of Kabbala in Palestine) and in Jerusalem took care to dress in white — certainly not in black or red, which would be prohibited by the regulating authority. They would go out of the town into open country converted by the arrival of the Schechina into that 'holy apple-field' (garden of fertility). This excursion represents a procession to fetch the bride whom they go to meet. Special hymns and joyful psalms would be sung — such as Psalm 29, or 95 to 99. The most famous of these hymns ('Go, my beloved, to meet the bride')... links mystical symbolism closely with the messianic hope of bringing the Schechina home from exile, and it is still sung today in every synagogue... Isaak Luria explained it as 'rich in mystical meaning' and especially to be recommended on returning home to greet one's mother. One then went round the table in a ceremonial circle, in silence and taking from the table two bunches of myrtle for the bride and bridegroom, and then singing a greeting to the angels who according to the Talmud lead people home at the beginning of the Sabbath.[13]

Now the praise of the woman of valour [i.e. the Schechina] must be interrupted for a little as the Schechina is invoked and invited to take part in this Sabbath meal with a 'holy elder'. Finally the solemn call rings out in Aramaic:

> Prepare the feast of perfect faith
> To please the holy King
> Prepare the feast of the King!
> Here is the feast of the holy apple-field...

Since in any case the Song of Songs, as marriage hymn of the divine bride (Schechina), forms the basis of Sabbath evening recitation, the nature of the Sabbath as symbolizing a wedding is thereby underlined. This ceremony also helps us to understand the sacramental-erotic allusions which, like a mystic religion, are found in a Sabbath hymn which merges earthly and heavenly marriage in a sacramental unity. Here the 'holy apple' (the magic Duda'im, mandragora or 'love berry') must be invoked if the husband wishes to embrace his wife to the fullest extent and utterly fulfil her. So also the fish for the Friday meal must be especially chosen because it is eaten on the eve of the Sabbath as a symbol of fertility. From this comes the regulation about eating fish on a Friday. All these things are described quite literally in a hymn that has a permanent place in Kabbalistic Sabbath ritual:

> I sing in hymns of the way to the gates
> To the apple-field, which are holy.
>
> Now we prepare a new table for her
> A beautiful candlestick sheds light overhead
>
> The bride comes between right and left
> In hallowed adornment and festive garments
>
> Her husband embraces her to the fullest extent
> Gives her satisfaction, presses home with all his strength
>
> Agonies and cries are raised
> Now faces, minds and spirits are made new
>
> He brings her joy in twofold measure
> Light shines forth and blessings flow
>
> The bride's attendant, step in and prepare the bride
> Many different dishes and all kinds of fish
>
> To create souls and new spirits.
>   . . .

I turn the mystical candlestick to the South
With the bread on the table I allow space to the North

With the wine in the cup and myrtle branches
The betrothed pair are strengthened against weakness

We bind crowns for them from precious words
About the fifty to seventy gates

The Schechina is surrounded by six Sabbath loaves
On every side joined to the One above.[14]

The realization of divine union on the Sabbath thus has its effect on mankind's craving for unity and completeness. Sabbath joy, we see, has a double aspect: both male and female sexual desires are clearly brought out in the *Sefer ha-Zohar*:

For the joy of married union is a blissful (religious) duty, and as such is the joy of the Schechina... for if a man is not considerate to his wife he sins, because in so doing he betrays the honour of the higher union which his wife has made possible for him. However, if his wife becomes pregnant, then a holy spirit is sent down out of the higher union. And so this marriage contract becomes known as a 'marriage of the All-holy'. Therefore devotion is necessary in the rapture of love as it is in the rapture of the Sabbath, which is the married union of the believer... then they would please their spouses for the glory of the heavenly union and in order to devote their hearts to the will of God.[15]

The *Sefer ha-Zohar* gives a similar answer when asked: 'When can man be called one, i.e. fulfilled?' The answer is entirely governed by the *mysterium coniunctionis*:

In the hour when man and wife live in heavenly holiness, and their soul is directed towards sanctification. In that hour when husband and wife are in physical union in the lawful manner, in the way of sanctification, then they will be whole and can be called *one* without stain on their being. In this hour the man will rejoice with his wife, in unity of will with her, both as one, directed towards their goal. When they are in such unity it is a oneness of body and soul. Of the soul — because one affects the other in unity of will. Of the body — because, as we are taught, a person not married is a being split asunder. Only when man and wife are joined and become one spirit and one flesh, will they be called one. In this way is the Almighty one with us, and he sends the Holy Ghost to each 'one'.[16]

6

Mystical Marriage

Mysticism, that intense kind of religious experience that can be participated in but which defies definition, has as its aim, in all its many manifestations, the possibility of meeting God and above all of being united with Him (*unio mystica*). So in this sense *mysterium coniunctionis*, and with it holy or mystical marriage, is to be identified as the true theme of mysticism, regardless of what form or historical expression it may take.

On the central question of how the 'Fall', i.e. the condition of man separated from God, may be redeemed, the anonymous Frankfurt author of the so-called *Theologia Deutsch* says:

> If it is to come to pass, then God must become human *within me*, so that God takes unto Himself all that is in me, within as well as without, so that there may be in me nothing repugnant to God, that would hinder His work. If He takes all mankind unto Himself, those who are here now and those who have been, and if He becomes human in them and they become divine in Him, and if then this should not happen also to me, then my fall and my separation would never be redeemed, and would continue *in me*.[1]

One thing emerges clearly from this passage: its author (we may generalize and say the Christian mystic) takes very seriously the condition of lacking in grace in which man finds himself. And since separation from God is said to affect everyone, and yet is not accepted as an unalterable fate, there is consequently a great longing to overcome it and to bridge the gap between God and man. So a bridging process on a large scale takes place, although this vital remedy or 'improvement' cannot be accomplished on man's part. This, at least, is the conviction of the *Theologia Deutsch*. For in Chapter 3 it continues:

> Towards my improvement and reform I neither can, nor may, nor

should, do anything other than simply to cry aloud my suffering, so that God alone may do and move all things in me, and I may submit to him and all His works and His divine will...[2]

It is certainly no accident that Martin Luther, after he had been granted the reforming revelation that changed his life — 'by grace alone' — published this anonymous mystical work on two occasions (in 1516 and 1518), and strongly recommended it to his friends as a kind of clue to the mystery.[3]

Further, Chapter 14 of *Theologia Deutsch* allows us to follow our theme more closely. In it the anonymous author draws the reader's attention to a 'three-step-way' of the Christian mystic, that is, that of purification (*catharsis*), of enlightenment (*illuminatio*) and of union (*unio mystica* or mystical marriage). He writes:

Purification belongs to *beginners* or penitents and comes about in three ways: with repentance and sorrow for sin, with full confession, and with full atonement... Enlightenment belongs to those *improving* and also comes about in three ways: in turning away from sin, in practising virtue and good works, and in bearing patiently with all temptation and adversity... Union concerns the *perfected* person and also comes about in three ways: in purity and integrity of the heart, in love of God and in contemplation [i.e. in vision] of God, the Creator of all things.[4]

So it appears that for our 'Frankfurt Sage' the ethical factor is the most important, while the speculative factor, though operating at the height and depth of spiritual experience, remains in the background. This is not typical of the didactic message of medieval mystics. It is a question of whether even the boldest definitions and the most glowing descriptions of what is experienced are sufficient to express the inexpressible — the immensity of numinous mystical experience. Dante's words are relevant here (*Divine Comedy, Paradise* 3.I.70):

> Rapture I felt. What it may be
> Words do not reveal...

Or:

> No words describe
> Such heavenly profusion.

There seems (paradoxically) no limit set for such 'heavenly profusion' since initiates to the mystery (men or women) are in the last analysis not satisfied to understand their relationship with the divine simply as a form of 'friendship with God'.[5] If we are to take seriously the often inflamed 'ecstatic confessions' which attempt to express the inexpressible, to put ideas into metaphorical language, then their only possible means of expression lies finally in the symbolic world of Eros. So it was for the Greek mystic Simeon, on whom the title of new theologian was conferred, in his invocation of God as 'the Erotic', that is, in a love song to God, when he wrote:

Come, you who have longed and longed for my poor soul. Come solitary one to him who is alone. For I am alone as you see. Come, you who have cut me off and made me alone on Earth. Come, my desire, to one you have created, whom I beseech, whom no one may command. Come my breath, my life. Come rejoicing and in glory and a continual delight!... Loving Lord raise then a tent in me, and dwell in me, and leave me not until I quit this Earth and separate not from me![6]

Similar examples of God's companionship and longing for God can be found in other religions, for example mystical Islam. But because of the Old Testament imagery of God's betrothal with His bride Israel, there is only a small step from Simeon, who wrote about the year 1000, to the medieval mystery of the bride. It was natural and unavoidable that the image of human love and marriage should appear to the mystic as the best of parallels for the 'fulfilment of his life', for the surrender of his soul, first to the call and finally to the embrace of total love. 'This allegory was close at hand so to speak; it was universally understood and moreover offered at a lower level a remarkably exact parallel with the sequence of events in which mankind's religious awareness developed and which determined the whole development of mystical life.[7]

It also penetrates to the innermost, most intensive form of experience of the soul in union with God. Unreserved loving dedication, the spiritual intimacy of which cannot be disturbed by anything external or earthly, could not be expressed in any other words than those of the erotic — however great the contrast with the ascetic disposition of some Christian mystics in particular cases. Is it then surprising that the Song of Songs held a privileged place in the reading and meditation of medieval mystics? Again and again the Song of Songs is extolled as the subject of allegorical interpretation. In this context the name of Bernard of Clairvaux comes first to mind. By his time (in the eleventh century) the subject of the bride and marriage was no longer new.[8] Nevertheless, this ardent, crusading priest was to become the real father of the Christian bride mystery:

He was the first to see the passionate love poetry of the Song of Songs as symbolic of the ever-changing experiences of a mystery charged with emotion... The Pauline relationship with the risen Lord through prayer, becomes a tenderly enjoyable communion with a heavenly bridegroom through love, from which the Song of Songs derived its fantasy-filled images and vivid symbols. Mystical life in the seclusion of a Catholic monastery was fed upon St Bernard's mystery of the Redeemer...[9]

This devoutness is also noticeable in the wealth of Protestant songs, both baroque and pietistic. We must remember in this connection that for St Bernard marriage and death — sacramental union with Christ and union with the suffering of the Passion — are closely related. In his mystical preaching on the Song of Songs (*Sermones in Cantica Canticorum*) his ideas revolve round the divine word and the human soul, symbolized as bride and bridegroom. For example when St Bernard takes a phrase from the Song of Songs — 'Let him kiss me with the kisses of his mouth' (1:2) — this is the explanation that accompanies it:

Who is it, who speaks these words? It is the bride. Who is the bride? It is the soul thirsting after God... She who desires this is bound with a bond of love to Him from whom she desires it. Of all natural feelings love is the most wonderful, especially when it returns to its beginning and source, that is to God. Nothing expresses mutual love between God's word and the soul so delightfully as the words 'bridegroom' and 'bride'. For those who stand in such a relationship to each other hold everything in common; nothing is held separately or for him — or herself alone. They have *one* heir, *one* house, *one* table, *one* bed and are in truth *one* flesh... If it is seemly for a bridegroom and bride to love one another, then it cannot be unseemly to give the loving soul the name of bride.[10]

And in another part of his sermon on the Song of Songs:

Blessed the soul that feels so sweet an embrace! For it is not less than pure holy love, tender sweet love, love that is joyous and true, inner shared love that joins two not in one flesh but two in one spirit, and leaves not two as two, but makes two into *one*. As Paul has said (1

Corinthians 6.17), 'But he that is joined unto the Lord is one spirit.'[11]

St Bernard does not neglect to warn those who long for mystical union with God against an in any way physical interpretation of a purely spiritual event. For:

We can only express in semblance from afar, only in our poor words, what happens in the pure spirit when it is taken up by God — or when God is pleased to enter into our very soul we must seek out the spiritual in a truly spiritual way, for this union takes place in the spirit only, for God is but spirit not body...

So the images of the Song of Songs are transcended and transformed. It is only total submission to the will of God, which (as St Bernard says) 'unites the soul with Him... Know that such a soul is as a spouse to the eternal word of God: it has joined with Him in spirit.'[12]

And when in the end all talking about mystical experience must be put aside along with the allegories, the metaphors and the similes in order to become God's 'in spirit and truth', still the mystic is not free from the imagery of erotic love. The poetry of nuns in the thirteenth and fourteenth centuries provides many examples of 'brides' who have pledged themselves solemnly to the heavenly bridegroom. Chanting and singing of praise also started in convents at the time of the early medieval German love songs, and this was quite in keeping with the tone of the Song of Songs. These mystical nuns did not describe their visions and inner perceptions from the position of distant onlookers. They were themselves the blessed betrothed and spouses of their Lord. Not everyone could reach the spiritual heights and depths of Christ-like experience as Matilda of Magdeburg, who in a little book, *The Flowing Light of Divinity* describes her encounter with God in these lines:

> O rejoice in the vision,
> O joy, O blessed angel's greeting
> And blissful embrace!
> I am bewildered by thy wonders, O Lord,
> Your grace casts me down,
> So hidden art thou
> And so abidest heavenly rock,
> That only eagles nest in Thee,
> And nightingales and doves.[13]

And when Matilda receives 'God's body' in the consecrated

bread then 'the godhead unites with our blameless soul and God's manhood mingles with our flesh' — an experience that adds the quality of a mystical marriage to the taking of the sacrament. The bridal mystery lives on in the lives of many nuns, sometimes as the blessed experience of an inner uplifting, but not infrequently as a painful suffering, an experience that reaches into the psychosomatic but not to the extent of being psychopathological. At the same time, plainly one should not regard *unio mystica* or mystical marriage as aiming at such manifestations.

Christina Ebner from the convent of Engelthal near Nuremberg, who reported her life and visions in a short work, *Overloaded with Grace*, seems to have been completely enthralled by visions of becoming a bride. She has her heavenly bridegroom express himself thus:

I am your captive in love. I come to you with gladness. I will crown you with compassion. I am the conqueror of your soul... On Saturday he spoke to her: 'You are coming to a place where all your misery will be at an end. The holy stream which flows from me into saints and laity, flows also into you and out of you again.' On Sunday he said: 'I come to you as one who has died of love. I come to you as a husband to a bridal bed. I come to you with warmth of passion. I come as one giving great gifts.[14]

Even when the psychological aspect is taken into account in assessing the many expressions of mysticism from nuns, it should be said that one of the greatest mystics, Richard of Saint-Victor (mid-twelfth century) took the symbolism of mystical marriage very seriously. In *De Quatuor Gradibus Violentiae Charitatis* [The Four States of Passionate Love], he describes the 'steep steps of love' and differentiates between four stages. These are betrothal, wedding, the married state, and finally fruitfulness of the contemplative being, within marriage and through and in God. This great mystical theologian allows for no doubt that union given from 'above' forbids any vulgarization of the wedding ceremony. Basically all true mystics are at one of this point. They agree with St Teresa of Avila, the most important Spanish mystic of the sixteenth century, who testified to her alarm as well as her happiness at the experience of being a bride of Christ. Yet at the same time she solemnly stressed that she could not reveal more about this mystery.

Yet mystics of all periods have felt obliged to share with con-

temporaries and with posterity the plentiful evidence on which
they have drawn, in addition to their own experience. They
have necessarily followed the Flemish Jan van Ruysbroeck, the
hermit of Groenendal, who in the second half of the fourteenth
century described 'the honour of spiritual espousal' as he saw it:

> This quintessential union of our spirit with God does not happen
> by itself, but belongs to God, flows from God, is entwined with God,
> and returns to God as its eternal cause. It is not separated from God,
> neither with its unique quality does it abandon God.[15]

> This meeting and union, overwhelming and immediate, which the
> loving spirit attains in God, must take place in our deepest essence,
> hidden from intellectual reasoning and in the innocence and under-
> standing of grace. In this richly joyful union must we rest, beyond
> ourselves and beyond all things.[16]

At this juncture, when the soul belongs wholly to God, all that
can be said to describe mystical marriage becomes relevant once
more. Thus the language of the bridal mystery finds its way
into the writings of Martin Luther. To be sure, the evidence
of mystical marriage was not important to him as a reformer.
But he was well acquainted with the metaphor of the human
soul as a bride.[17] In his revolutionary key work, *Of the Freedom
of a Christian Man* (1520) he wrote that belief 'unites the soul
with Christ as a bride to her groom'; by this Luther equates
belief with a wedding ring symbolizing the fellowship of Christ
and the believer. Whereas Bernard of Clairvaux saw the
individual soul as the bride of Christ, Luther put more stress
on the image of the bride as symbolizing rather the Christian
world and Christian doctrine. In a sermon in 1537 it was put
like this:

> Among all the picturesque allegories which God has given us to por-
> tray the Kingdom of Christ, one delightful, affectionate image is the
> comparison of Christendom or the Christian faith with a wedding,
> a holy matrimony in which God chooses a Church for His Son to
> take for his own as a bride.[18]

Christ is thus made a party to a wedding contract — his being
becomes part of a *mysterium coniunctionis*, something that is
qualitatively far more than merely being part of a tax-paying
body. . .
    Luther abandoned the image of the bride-and-marriage mys-
tic, binding herself like a nun in mystical betrothal and wed-

ding with a heavenly bridegroom, when he came more and
more to use the comparison of a household in which the housewife becomes wholly occupied in 'happy housekeeping'.
Already in *Of the Freedom of a Christian Man* we have a description brought down to the common daily round.

Is it not a happy household in which the bridegroom Christ, rich,
noble and pious, takes as bride a wanton woman, poor despised and
evil, frees her from all sin and showers her with good things?

And elsewhere, in a sermon in 1522:

Love will be evil and marriage ill-wrought, should the bridegroom
not give his bride the keys and control over wine and bread and
household things... In Christian faith it is given that Christ is the
bridegroom and I am the spouse. His is the kingdom, his the piety,
righteousness, purity, wisdom and patience, likewise all God's mercy
and grace are his. Therefore these things which are my bridegroom's
are indeed also mine. As Paul says also in Romans 8:32: 'He that
spared not his own Son, but delivered him up for us all, how shall
he not with him also freely give us all things?[19]

Admittedly, with this development the central theme, that mysticism was a special means of experiencing God intensely, was
abandoned and the mystical setting of sacred marriage was
given up. We find instead a wedding situation in the style of
Pieter Brueghel. This change of presentation, however,
represents no loss; indeed it stresses the scope and extent of
the symbol of a wedding. We should remember in this connection that what is experienced within has to find its way out
to the workaday world and submit to the test of everyday living. No less a person than Master Eckhart recognized this when
he spoke less of mystical marriage than of an inner, loving
encounter and of the 'birth of God in the depths of the soul'.

    The metaphor of the bride and the wedding retains its intrin-
sic value, however, and serves to suggest, as does no other
imagery, the deep, sudden contact with God, the feeling of
being embraced by God. The 'love storm' of Matilda of Magdeburg also is no empty allegorical aid to interpretation but
can only be described as bursting with strong, bewildered emotion. Hence Matilda's confession:

More I cannot write, nor should I; I see with the eyes of my soul
and hear with the ears of my eternal spirit and in all parts of my body
feel the power of the Holy Ghost.

Alois M. Haas makes this comment:

The absolute binding force of this medieval experience can be measured only by risking the use of daring profane erotic imagery, especially when one thinks of the fundamental difficulty of describing
mystical experience in formal language. The unsuitability of apply-
ing symbolism to sacred concepts means that finally the imagery is
overtaxed and breaks down, but despite the incompleteness and
inadequacy which adheres to the allegory of brideship, it offers after
all the possibility of expressing the inexpressible. It would be a mis-
take to think that the mystic was no longer dependent on linguistic
models: on the contrary he was still so to a high degree, for it is only
through linguistic indicators that break through speech that he could
point to his experience.[20]

One thing remains to hold on to as the special characteristic
of mystical marriage, namely, that it happens 'inwardly' in a
state of broad extra-corporeal awareness and that in practice
it goes beyond the scope of even the best description. The great
Spanish mystic St Teresa of Avila wrote and bore witness to
this in her *Interior Castle (Moradas del Castillo Interior):*

There is one great difference above others between visions of the
earlier dwelling place [i.e. 'the interior castle'] and those which belong
to this last dwelling place. . . I have already said that this spiritual
betrothal has as little to do with the body as if the soul had been separated from it and become pure spirit. This is still more true of spiritual
marriage because this union full of mystery (*Matrimonio espiritual*) takes
place in the inner sanctum of the soul, where God himself dwells
and where, as I think, he goes in and out without doors.[21]

7

Jakob Böhme and Marriage with the Divine Sophia

The great theme of spiritual marriage and the spiritual bride was celebrated by Jakob Böhme — who was, according to Schelling, that 'natural theogonist and genius in the history of man' — in unexpected ways. His work was astonishing in two respects. In the first place it is surprising that in the century after the Reformation a Lutheran Christ should be allowed to reveal the female principle in the Christian image of God. The fundamentally one-sided and puritanical philosophy of Protestantism had turned out to be stubbornly long-lasting, and not to be softened by any influence from the mystically-coloured worship of Mary, which Luther had known in his youth and later years.[1] Indeed the Reformer of Wittenberg not only gave an interpretation of the hymn in praise of Mary (*Magnificat*, 1521) (called by Bernhard Lohse that 'pearl of Luther's Bible') that was sensitive and clearly inspired by the German mystical spirit, but he also preached a good sixty sermons on the feast days of Mary, which he celebrated all his life.[2] But in the years that followed, hardly anything of this ostensibly 'Catholic' Luther remained in the tradition of the Lutherans. That is one point.

The other point especially worth noting is how, at the beginning of the seventeenth century, a simple yet brilliant shoemaker from Görlitz suddenly produced a wholly new view of mystical marriage, and how through him the divine Sophia (Wisdom) was made accessible to man in two forms: on one hand in God's creation, in which divine wisdom is, so to speak, reflected; and on the other hand in an inner individual process, to be understood as 'Christo-Sophia', a way to Christ in which marriage takes place with the virgin Sophia. For Böhme this marriage was the centre and high point of mystical experience;

it is also, however, a symbol of man's recovery of his original wholeness, a likeness to God's image that man had lost at the fall of Adam. Franz von Baader, the nineteenth-century authority on Böhme, has called this Christo-sophistical aspect, or marriage with Sophia, the true 'reintegration of mankind'. As with the gnostics and German mystics, this marriage had to do with mankind itself. It expresses the secret aim of finding oneself.

We may assume that Jakob Böhme took his ideas from the rich religio-historical material that was available at least in the Bible in the early seventeenth century. It should not be forgotten either, that he was open to other influences, such as the Jewish Kabbala and that of the alchemists, since they were part of the background of a spiritually enlightened person at the time of the Thirty Years' War. Even though he was a shoemaker and not formally well-educated, Böhme drew on another first-hand source [3] when he wrote:

My knowledge does not bring together words from many books, but I have words *within me*. For Heaven and Earth are essentially within us, including God himself. Cannot a man read in the book that he is? If I had no other book than my own, the one that I am myself, then I have books enough. So if I have the whole Bible *within me* — then I have Christ's spirit. [4]

Böhme's work is not based on a tradition of passing on knowledge. Rather it comes from an immediacy of spiritual vision, in which the Görlitz master's writing is as wide-ranging as it is deeply grounded. Whoever studies Chapter 19 of Böhme's famous first work, *Aurora or The Rising Sun* (1612), will find how closely his testimony about marriage with the virgin Sophia is fused with his own spiritual experience. This enables him to report from the critical standpoint of his own inner doubts and struggles:

...immediately after several emotional storms, my spirit broke through the gates of Hell to the godhead born within me, and I was encompassed by love *as a beloved bride is embraced by her bridegroom*. Just what a spiritual triumph this was I cannot write or tell. It cannot be compared with anything except being given *life in the midst of death*, indeed it was as life for one who had risen from the dead. [5]

Again there is no metaphor equal to that of a loving embrace to express the special quality of this inner experience in figurative language. And again we see images of marriage and death in close proximity. 'Death is invited to the wedding', Novalis will say later from another perspective. What a powerful archetype lies at the heart of the symbol of married union for it repeatedly to stir people to the depths and to change them! And Jakob Böhme writes as one deeply moved, who has been through a spiritual change described as wedding with the virgin Sophia.

First, though, who is the divine Sophia or Wisdom? The answers which have been given for more than 2,000 years come from a chorus of many voices. St Augustine once wrote: 'We not only recognize but openly proclaim, that the highest wisdom in God is the communion whereby each soul may be given wisdom and become truly wise.'

But the concept ranges more widely than this. The divine Sophia is a special feature of the Eastern Orthodox Church. Our picture of Sophia to a large extent follows its teaching on the subject — 'Sophiology'. And yet that is not the whole story.[6] We have already met an image of Sophia in late-Jewish biblical tradition, where she is presented as a female figure in direct touch with God. She, Wisdom, is an agent of the Creator: 'The Lord by wisdom hath founded the earth' (Proverbs 3:19). With her He prepared Heaven and Earth. We think of the Wisdom of the Old Testament, of the Old Testament Apocrypha, and of the proverbial 'Wisdom of Solomon'. Whoever follows traces of the divine Sophia through the history of religious dogma may be surprised to find that the cult of Sophia developed in the Roman Catholic Church earlier than the cult of the Virgin Mary. The early witnesses of the divine Sophia speak of this 'intimate companion' of God from an inner experience and in a state of spiritual emotion. To quote the early Christian writer Laktanz: 'We receive Sophia and bear witness that, coming from God, she must be welcomed by each and every one of us.' Once again marriage communion is emphasized as it is in St Augustine's interpretation of the Psalms:

Wisdom offers herself freely to us all; yet she is for everyone pure and unsullied. Mankind will be changed by her, but for everyone she remains unchanged. No earthly or even heavenly beauty, no embrace or lying together, can be compared with the beauty, sweetness, inspiration and pleasure of Wisdom. Whoever wishes to love, let him therefore love Wisdom. Let him woo her that he may come to her. As a lover's eye lusts after his beloved, so a pure heart seeks for her.

St Basil the Great sought to raise Sophia's veil of secrecy when he wrote:

> The soul follows its instinct when it comes to meet Wisdom and embraces her like an ardent lover. As Solomon said: love her so she may caress you. The body may be sullied by impure endearments but in the embrace of Wisdom, when the whole soul is united utterly and blended with her, then it will be filled and made pregnant with holiness and purity. [7]

As for the theme of mystical marriage as we encounter it in the writings of Jakob Böhme, we shall now put on one side that aspect of Sophia that relates to the cosmos: the divine Sophia as emanation and mirror ('meditation') of the Holy Trinity, as it is experienced finally in all creation. In our context it is the anthroposophical aspect of the divine Sophia, i.e. that related to the understanding of humanity and its development, that is of special interest. For here is something that will recover man's lost ideal, his spiritual wholeness. This is the real goal of married union to which Böhme constantly refers, for example when he describes the origin and fall of Adam in his great commentary on Genesis, the *Mysterium Magnum*, or when in *Christosophia* he points the way to a spiritual change leading to union with one's own lost centre, that is, with the virgin Sophia. Marriage and change belong together!

Also, at the core of Jakob Böhme's anthropological ideas there lies a great secret. It is the mystery of androgyny, the male-female principle inherent in the wholeness[8] of humanity. Although Böhme's thinking was sparked off by his personal spiritual visions, his contribution to the question of androgyny cannot be separated from the mainstream of spiritual history. He maintains that man (as in the famous passage in Genesis 1:27) was created 'male *and* female'. According to Böhme's *Mysterium Magnum*: 'Adam was a man and also a woman... in him were *both* elements of fire and light, and in their union was the pure heart of devoted love.' [9] And he continued:

> In Adam were two fixed and changeless beings: the spiritual body, the love-essence of innermost Heaven which was God's temple; and the outer body, the dust and ashes of Earth, which was the outer

shell of the spirit. The outer body in no way shared the futility [i.e. transitoriness] of Earth, and it would be freed from the Devil's curse of transience and corruption at the Last Judgment. These same two beings, that is, the inner heavenly and the outer heavenly, were united with each other, and conceived in one body, a *single body* but with two kinds of essence.[10]

This androgynous archetype of male-female wholeness has

Figure 4: The Crucifixion of Christ shown as *coniunctio* of sun and moon. (Late ninth century. Paris, Bibliothèque Nationale. From Edward F. Edinger, *The Anatomy of the Psyche*, La Salle, Illinois, 1986.)

been broken up. Böhme divined the existence of this lost archetype and its destruction. But his gaze was directed forward to
the future and to the life of Christ and his sufferings for
mankind. He envisaged Christ not only as the Redeemer, but
also as one who, at the same time, by restoring what had been
lost, could finally make whole the broken androgynous archetype. Christ's sacrifice was consequently a valid answer to the
longing of divided human nature for the eternal, for fulfilment,
for becoming whole. The procreative instinct and sexual desire
suitably express this unquenchable longing and they also seek
to satisfy it, but without being able to do so in the long run.
They remain powerful symbols, points of reference or
metaphors of a temporary nature. All the same, indeed because
they are temporary, their language and metaphors enable someone such as Jakob Böhme to put into words this deep human
longing for *unio* or *communio,* joining together God and human:
'This is a great mystery. . .' (Ephesians 5:32). Or, in the words
of Jakob Böhme:

So nature craves the eternal and longs to have done with futility (transience). And so arises in the male and female of all creatures the strongest desire to intermingle one with another; but the flesh cannot
comprehend it, neither does the breath of the spirit. Only the two
elements together, male and female, they comprehend it.[11]

Böhme continues:

When Christ on the Cross once more redeemed man's virgin male-
female image, and coloured it with heavenly blood in divine love,
when he had done this he exclaimed: 'It has come to pass. . .' Christ
changed the sleeping Adam from being man and woman, back to
his original angelic image. Great and wonderful are these mysteries
that the world is unable to grasp.[12]

For Böhme, this resort to the myth of androgyny had two con-
sequences: for one thing it enabled him to understand, and to
make clear, the loss of a male-female archetype, and for another
to show that sexual union can be only an image and a promise
of the 'great mystery' represented by Christ and his Church
(according to Ephesians 5:32). With this background, the concept of androgyny becomes the way, indeed the most sensible
way, to understand union with Christ on the path to
'Christosophia'. This does not imply anything like a theological instructional treatise on the wisdom of Christ, but rather
a Christian initiation leading to inner experience of Christ, ena-

bling us to follow him through the stages of Passion, Death and Resurrection, or his rising from the dead. As it says in one of Böhme's Christosophical tracts: 'If you would draw close to him (Christ), then you must know him in wholeness, from his Incarnation to his Ascension. For only then will the virgin Sophia be wedded to the soul.' [13] In other words, to become whole as a human being, as fundamentally it is in everyone's nature to be, is to prepare oneself for marriage with the divine Sophia. She embodies (for man) that inner spiritual feminine, which was lost through the fall, and became a divided sexuality.

Franz von Baader, who, as mentioned above, became in his day the interpreter of Jakob Böhme (i.e. for Hegel, Schelling and the Romantics), expounded the framework of his erotic philosophy thus:

When I am shown a Christian, I am shown a person who is in the process of reintegration, and when I am shown a person engaged in reintegration I am shown a Christian. It is of the highest importance, especially in our time, to set out plainly this concept of Christianity as integrated humanity, and only that theology which presents sin as disintegration, and redemption and rebirth as human reintegration, will prevail over its opponents. [14]

These words of the philosopher already look forward, since they bring into the open a concept that the ancient gnostics and the medieval mystics had left formulated in similes and parables, and which Theresa of Avila, though admitting to it ('in mystical marriage I have experienced union'), had not allowed herself to talk about.

Not so Jakob Böhme. Assailed on many sides and taken to task, he saw himself frequently obliged to answer his hostile critics as well as his spiritually like-minded friends and pupils. [15] In his *Second Defence against Balthasar Tilke* (1621) he gives an answer related to the origin of his knowledge of wisdom. For example: 'God has given me knowledge. The I who am 'I' does not know it, but God knows it in me.' [16] And since now Wisdom is God's bride and the children of Christ live in God's wisdom, then they are also brides of God; in the same way as branches of vines are organically bound to Christ who is the grapevine. There follows Böhme's further question: 'Should I not then know the spirit of Christ from which the world was made, since he who made it and lives in me, must he not know it?' In other words, union with God and with

Christ makes mankind a receptacle of wisdom and a bearer of spiritual knowledge. Thus the craftsman of Görlitz, however humble his station, whatever his limits, could display astonishing self-knowledge and an insight that shows a deep spiritual perception of the *mysterium coniunctionis*. From this knowledge he was able to answer his critics:

My soul is *His* (i.e. God's or Christ's wife in whom *He* begets knowledge in the measure that *He* wishes. Just as eternal wisdom is God's body and He begets whatever He will, so when He begets I do nothing, only *He in me*. I am as one inactive in the birth of higher knowledge, and He is my life. I have neither sought it nor learned it. He inclines to my being and my being inclines to Him.[17]

That is to say: whoever speaks about the marriage of Sophia has at times had personal inner experience of union and recognition. His knowledge of mystical marriage will come from this mystery and not from everyday, self-conscious, rational argument.

It follows that the divine Sophia or Wisdom is not only 'the eternal mother' and 'producer of all things', in whom the godhead is seen as in a mirror and allows itself to be reflected. She is not only the bride of the divine Word *(logos)* and the 'eternal manifestation of holy word and will', but she is also part of the archetypal essence of mankind itself. For 'God's wisdom was born through the gracious virgin in him (Adam) [i.e. the first man] and opened with her eyes Adam's soul . . . and the noble virgin and God's power were married with him.'[18]

This union with his heavenly Sophia went with wholeness of identity. Adam's tragic fall marked the beginning of an estrangement from self and God which was only to be revoked through Christ's death on the Cross. And even then a new marriage was needed. Böhme wrote not only as one with spiritual experience, but (something inseparable from it) as one with experience of sorrow. He makes a point of stressing in his Christosophical treatises that obstacles and setbacks occur 'on the difficult way to Christ' and to the virgin Sophia. It was a case of fighting under the banner of a brave order of knighthood 'for the noble garland of knights. . . and in this struggle the earthly, evil body [i.e. that which has lost its archetypal virtue] must be destroyed and vanish away.'[19]

Such determination can be finally justified only by the attraction of a virgin bride. At least two aspects are significant for

Böhme here: first there is the virgin Sophia who 'kisses' only the person who, as a knight, has come through the spiritual battle of an inner renewal while following in the steps of Christ. The other aspect arises when, in Revelation, one looked upon the 'wedding of the Lamb' and the great wedding feast as the ultimate goal for humanity. Böhme's description in his Christosophical writing is in accordance with an initiation, a Christ-like way of dedication which — as already suggested — begins with changing from the flesh and ends with ascent to heaven. Böhme also knows well the mood of joyful expectation and rejoicing before an approaching wedding, for 'the rising morning sun' has long been for him an inner certainty. But 'the way to Christ' which is supposed to culminate in union with the heavenly virgin, is first a path of affliction and testing. Therefore:

Dear soul, listen earnestly. This must not be a mere recital of words. This must be practised with a serious, sober will or it will not be achieved. For if the soul is to win Christ's knightly garland from the noble virgin Sophia, it must court her with the greatest passion of love... for she is the Rose of Sharon (in the Song of Songs) the rose in the valley with whom Solomon dallied and called his love, his demure virgin, whom he adored, as indeed have all holy men before and after him. Whoever has won her has called her his pearl.[20]

The Gospel parable of the priceless pearl and also the Song of the Pearl as it has come down to us in the gnostic Acts of Thomas, belongs in the broad context of this description by the Master of Görlitz.

So Jakob Böhme shows at the very heart of his work what pride of place he gives to mystical marriage, man's way to his true self. Christ is the guarantor and representative of this self through Sophia, bringing back the likeness of God to a corrupt humanity. Adam's bride (before the Fall) and Christ's bride basically represent man himself reborn.

In other words, as Ernst Benz says:

Christ is inborn in every soul as he was in Mary, so that the soul is infused with heavenly wisdom, and by marriage Christ the bridegroom is made fruitful. This fundamental androgynous oneness of Christ which exists in his eternal union with Sophia, is the basis of many different expressions of the religious experience of *unio*. Union with him can be so variously described that Christ may appear as bridegroom or as bride. He is the bridegroom when he is the spouse of Sophia, the heavenly likeness of God; he is the bride when he is the heavenly image that marries the soul. He is a bridegroom as a man when joining a soul of light, but a heavenly young bride when joining a soul of fire. One is hidden in the other. One is present in the other. What is definite, however, is that this marriage does not take place in some distant universe but in mankind itself.[21]

We must fully agree with this dictum of the religious historian who adopted Jakob Böhme's interpretation. But what does it really mean to say that the union of Christ and Sophia takes place 'in man'? It is obviously not referring to physical fact. It is also not enough just to gather together relevant texts and images, if these cannot advance the spiritual reality of mystical marriage and the fundamental truth on which the longing of mankind for self-realization and wholeness ultimately rests. At least Jakob Böhme has given us a strong spiritual lead, an historic clarion call:

Dear soul, you must be ever earnest! You will receive the tender passion of a kiss from the noble Sophia in the holy name of Jesus; for she stands at the door of the soul and knocks and warns the sinner of his godless ways. Therefore once he desires her love, she is willing and will kiss him with the radiance of her sweet affection, bringing joy to his heart. But she will not lie down at once in the marriage bed beside the soul, for it will take her time to restore the bright image of heaven which faded in the Garden of Eden. [22]

Appendix: The Myth of Androgyny

'The myth of androgyny is the one great human myth on which anthropological metaphysics can be built.'[1] Nikolai Alexandrovitch Berdyayev's observation turns our attention to a combination of image and idea that promises to shed light on an important point in mystical marriage. For androgyny refers us back to the original state of mankind; at the same time it sheds light on the condition of humanity in a state of perfection. So being androgynous (from the Greek: *anér*, man, and *gyné*, woman) says something about both the archetype of mankind and its spiritual future. Accordingly it would be the function of mystical marriage to validate man's lost image, to maintain it, and to restore it.

Androgyny presents us with an image of mankind in a mythical past when man was not divided into male and female, but when there was a pre-sexual and super-sexual oneness. He was androgynous, that is, male *and* female. Sexual differentiation came about, the myth says, as a result of special circumstances, perhaps a tragic break or fall causing the problems of sex with all its accompanying manifestations. This is to be understood as the reason why men and women long to overcome their separation through sexual intercourse and to restore — if only for a moment — their original unity. This myth can be regarded as a key with which to unlock a simple puzzle of human existence.[2]

So androgyny is 'a special means of uniting the male and female principles in one person.'[3] And because Greek mythology saw Hermaphrodite, the son of Hermes and Aphrodite, as having the characteristics of both sexes and being bisexual, so hermaphrodite and androgynous are sometimes used as synonyms. That may be all right so long as one is talking about a mythical figure of speech for male-female wholeness, or sexual wholeness. But otherwise the hermaphrodite presents a physiological abnormality. As such it has nothing to do with the idea intended here of uniting male and female — such abnormality is quite outside our discussion.[4]

Mircea Eliade points out:

In the classical world the hermaphrodite represented an ideal condition and men sought, with the help of initiatory rites, to attain this state in a spiritualized form. But if at birth a child showed any hermaphrodite malformation it was killed by its parents. The anatomically deformed hermaphrodite was seen as an aberration of nature, as a sign of the gods' anger, and was consequently destroyed out of hand. Only ritual androgyny represented an ideal model, since it did not bring with it any abnormal organs, but had significance, seen symbolically, for the union of magical-sacred powers which both sexes have within them.[5]

From *this* symbolic point of view the hermaphrodite is a unifying model *par excellence*. According to C. G. Jung:

Unconcerned by his monstrosity, the hermaphrodite has gradually become a benefactor who heals conflicts, a significance he acquired in relatively early stages of civilization. This vital role explains why the hermaphrodite image did not die out in antiquity but, on the contrary, maintained its position down the centuries with increasing richness of symbolic content. The fact that so archaic a concept grew to such importance, points not only to the vitality of archetypal ideas generally, but demonstrates the soundness of the principle that the archetype mediates between conscious and unconscious elements *in uniting opposites*. It builds a bridge between the conscious present threatened with alienation and the natural unconscious unity of olden times.[6]

Without going into the wider psychological implications here, let us look at a range of manifestations in which hermaphrodite-androgynous symbols appear. The parallelism, or at any rate the close contiguity of mystical marriage symbols, is obvious. For just as god and goddess (or their human representatives) consummate *Hieros Gamos* in myths or rites to make nature fertile, so many cosmogonic gods appear in an androgynous form. Having both male and female qualities raises the participants to the stature of world creators. We have only to think of the eternal cohabitation of Shiva with his female counterpart Sati as a universal healing wholeness, towards which the Eastern believer confidently looks. (Westerners have a problem when they find the countless representation of the erotic-sacred act on the façades of Indian

Figure 5: The classical Indian Shriyantra, the expression of the spiritual union of opposites. (From C. G. Jung, *Grundwerk*, vol. 5, p. 104.)

temples 'improper' or 'obscene'.) From the many examples of opposites in union, let us cite here the classical Indian Shriyan-tra. This consists of a harmonious arrangement of upward and downward facing triangles which pierce one another or over-lap. Anybody who is meditating and concentrating on a par-ticular yantra (or mandala) can adapt it to the universal whole in question, and seek in meditation to establish this wholeness within himself — a kind of inner communion. It is not a mat-ter of neutralizing the two poles (Jakob Böhme calls them two 'tinctures') but rather of activating them in mystical marriage.

The recollection of an androgynous state in gods and men, is met with not only in Eastern religions, in ancient Egypt and among the early Germans, but also in ancient Greece. We are thinking here especially of Plato's *Symposium* which alludes to the original wholeness of men (Chapter 14). The account of the creation in Genesis (1:27) also refers to this phenomenon, even if it is hotly contested by theologians and in particular by ecclesiastical anthropologists. There is no doubt, however, that this passage in Genesis — 'male and female created he them' — came to have an androgynous interpretation for pre- and post-rabbinical late Jewry, for the Rabbis themselves, for Philo of Alexandria, in the Talmud, for the Kabbalists, and of course in gnostic writings.[7] There remains the future task of following the idea of androgyny from Plato and the more eso-teric interpretations of Genesis to the present day. The persis-tence of the idea of androgyny within modern Christianity is not to be denied, however strongly grounded the sexual differentiation of humanity into men and women and the per-sonal I-and-you relationship may be.[8]

In this connection Ernst Benz speaks of 'official suppression'. But the authorities were unable to prevent the idea of androgyny finding numerous exponents and interpreters. Among the most influential, as already shown, was Jakob Böhme, who included in his theo- cosmo- and Christo-sophy an 'anthropo-sophy' (human wisdom) which outlines a human male-female ideal and looks forward to the possibility of a spiritual restoration of this archetypal image, on the way to Christ and in 'marriage with the virgin Sophia' as the lost part of Adam's being. It is Böhme who makes it clear that the great theme of mystical marriage corresponds to a mental picture of androgyny. One symbol must not be thought to exclude the other. On the other hand we have the division of the (platonic) sphere-shaped androgynous archetype, giving man his individual 'ego', his ego-isolation, but also his capacity for love. On the other hand androgyny represents the ultimate goal for the ego that is separated from its deepest being, one that leads towards the restoration of a wholeness which is both possible and necessary. This archetypal beginning and this ultimate goal represent the two poles between which the life of mankind runs its course.

Jakob Böhme is not the only one who has seen humanity, and in particular its androgyny, in this light. There are the English followers of Böhme in the seventeenth century, the so-called Philadelphians, whose influence travelled back to the Continent. The two Swabian theosophers Friedrich Christoph Oetinger and Michael Hahn[9] were Böhme scholars, and the latter was spiritual head of a community named after Böhme which still exists in Württemburg today. Thanks to translations of the writings of the French theosopher and mystic Louis Claude de Saint-Martin[10] by, among others, Matthias Claudius, Böhme was 'rediscovered' in the era of German Romanticism and the idea of androgyny was taken up again. The name of Franz von Baader,[11] an all-round Catholic philosopher, can be quoted here as a representative example. To him, as to those like him, it was a matter of human 'reintegration'.

This ancient doctrine was brought into the present day by two Russian thinkers, Vladimir Solovyov and Nikolai Berdyayev.[12] The Sophiology of Eastern Orthodox Church teaching, and the ideas of Jakob Böhme, which found their way into Russia in the early nineteenth century through freemasonry among other means (also by means of Saint-Martin and Franz von Baader), blended with their own experiences, for Solovyov in particular. Not to be forgotten either are associations with the Rosicrucian alchemists, which we shall discuss separately. They cannot be properly understood without taking an androgynous whole image of man as a basis. Above all, this ancient belief is still active in our own day through the work of C. G. Jung, not in the sense of a simple continuance of old traditions, but rather as an aid to understanding the process of achieving spiritual maturity. In this alchemistic-symbolic or psychoanalytic sense, it is a matter of 'becoming *one*' and thus of approaching closer to self-realization.

Finally, according to the anthroposophy of Rudolf Steiner,

the concept of androgyny is an integral part of the great humanizing process of the incarnation. Although he has not presented it systematically, Steiner has referred in many places to the problem of androgyny.[13] If we wish to outline Steiner's views in a few words, the following picture emerges: at a certain stage — Steiner goes back to the formation of the planets before man walked on Earth — the splitting of human wholeness into the two sexes occurred. What at an earlier stage was enclosed in one person was from then on divided into two individuals. This 'individualization' took place in the service of increasing consciousness and the creation from within of an independent human ego. As Steiner looks at the history of the conscious in the broadest terms, this present-day sexual separation takes on a merely episodic character; for Steiner is looking not only back to a mythical image of archetypal androgynous man. but also forward to the farthest future of mankind.

Basically, the human ego already bears the mark of a supra-sexual wholeness, and therefore of real humanity in man. The further development of a mankind awakened to ego-consciousness leads on to an androgynous future image of humanity. This is an evolution which, of course, takes place very slowly. Steiner describes the outcome, to which there are many references, including biblical ones, thus:

The male soul in a female body and the female soul in a male body will become bi-sexual again, *being impregnated with the Holy Spirit*. Men and women are different in outward form; inwardly in both cases their spiritual one-sidedness will be merged together in a harmonious *whole*.[14]

Without doubt, as in other relevant references from his lectures, Steiner is dealing here with extremely difficult concepts, the interpretation of which leaves open many questions. We may be satisfied here with the observations that as with Jung — though there are differences in approach and terminology — he is dealing with a spiritual process of becoming whole. With Steiner this objective is not conceived only in a narrow anthropological sense, and not only with a view to achieving complete organic synthesis in *one* human life. Steiner reckons with the idea of karma and reincarnation. Looking ahead, he directs his gaze to the most distant horizon of mankind, so that he reaches common ground with the eschatological-apocalyptic testimony of the Bible.

8

A Discussion of Alchemy

As we have seen the theme of mystical marriage has gone through many changes of form in the course of time. This process is still going on today. But even if its signs and descriptions naturally alter, the innate force of this symbol persists. Its importance lies in the fact that as man's consciousness develops he comes more and more to understand that the apparently far-off myth of *Hieros Gamos* and the seemingly remote and obscure religious rites which relate to mystical marriage, refer in the end to a *coniunctio*, a fusing of opposites, to be set in train *in* mankind itself as a maturing process. More of this later.

When one considers religious and cultural history as the history of consciousness,[1] it appears that mystical marriage provides a kind of spiritual-historical bridge between the myths, especially the gnostic mysteries of early times, and modern possibilities of a broadening of consciousness. Such a bridge is formed by the images and practices of alchemy. Whereas adherents of earlier agricultural cultures aimed at ensuring the fruitfulness of their fields through the fertile, life-renewing co-operation of gods of vegetation, the alchemist was motivated by a different point of view. He saw it as his cultural mission to change the earth itself, by experimenting in handling material processes. This involved transmuting the base material of an original substance (*prima materia*) into a new quality. The supreme goal of this work lay in the preparation of a 'Philosopher's Stone' (*lapis philosophorum*). This involved transmuting the least valuable metal into the most valuable, i.e. into gold. The expert alchemist, however, knew the danger of perverting his undertaking. Hence the explicit statement: *'aurum nostrum non est aurum vulgi* — our gold is not ordinary gold, not pecuniary gold.'

There is no doubt, though, that gold-making and the associated investigation of the physical world was the great preoccupation of all alchemists. C. G. Jung, who worked for decades to shed light on changes produced by the opposite disciplines of alchemy and psychoanalysis, has called our attention to those pre-scientific researchers and technicians who may largely have been seeking an 'experience of the unknown'; one could also say, seeking for the spiritual in the material. And he went on:

One failed for so long to understand this side of alchemy — the *mystiká* — solely because nothing was known about psychology, in particular about the supra-personal and collective unconscious. So long as nothing is known of our psychic existence, when it does appear at all it will be as a speculation. So the first knowledge of spiritual laws or processes was thought to be in the stars and even more so in the alchemists' unknown matter. From both these speculative activities sciences have been developed — astronomy from astrology and chemistry from alchemy.[2]

The researchers working in alchemists' laboratories were trying to resolve the problem of opposites as it arose out of the opposition of spirit and matter. From this, mystical marriage comes into play in a modified form known as 'chemical marriage'. This sets a task which requires a response from the whole person, and not just technical knowledge and manual dexterity. Thus the state of mind in which a laboratory worker sets about his task is not unimportant. The success of the *'opus alchymicum'* will depend on his 'attitude' and also on his ethical-moral integrity. Reading treatises and looking at illustrations of alchemy brings out the relationship between *oratorium* and *laboratorium*, in other words — prayer and work! Looked at like this, the adept is not experimenting just with matter, but also all the time with himself. He himself is a sealed vessel. Self-realization gains a deeper meaning from this concept. The married union of opposites is arrived at inwardly as well as outwardly; it happens on the psychic as well as the physical level. Reality can only be experienced as *unus mundus,* one world.

For the alchemist as a person committed to this *unus mundus,* chemical processes in human terms had characteristics taken from life itself. The alchemist was handling not 'dead' matter but the very stuff of life. This material was subordinate to the sun (*sol*) or the moon (*luna*) and was accordingly coloured male or female. Describing this earlier understanding of reality, Mircea Eliade, an expert on religion, speaks frankly of a 'sexualized world' precisely because male and female qualities are manifested even in the material universe:

It depends how cosmic reality is presented and if it is seen as life itself, it will therefore be sexualized — for the special quality of all living being is sexuality. At a certain stage of culture the whole universe, including the world of 'nature' and even objects and man-made implements, was represented as sexualized... This view of the world came first, justifying various rituals, and then came the 'marriage of metals' through which alone 'birth' was possible. Similar ideas are to be found in ancient China. Yu, the great archetypal metal-worker, knew how to distinguish male metal from female. As a result he compared his cauldron to the two cosmological principles of Yin and Yang.[3]

It was only logical then for the *opus alchymicum*, 'the work', to go through stages in which the tincture matured and by which the Philosopher's Stone was brought to perfection according to the Hermetic principle: *solve et coagula* — dissolve and unite!

A central feature of the whole process was the fusing of sulphur and mercury. Both 'materials' were essences, or spiritual-material arcane substances, not to be confused with chemical elements in the modern sense. They must be understood as symbols and bearers of creative-procreative archetypal powers. For sulphur, corresponding to *sol*, the sun, was masculine and was personified as the 'King', while mercury (*mercurius*) corresponded to the moon, or the 'Queen', who was to be united with her husband. It should be noted that the astrological-alchemical sign for Mercury ☿ already showed a sign for union — a crescent moon touching the orb of the sun over a cross.

While the many symbolic representations handed down make clear the general working of the process, there are also innumerable variations in showing the phenomenon of conjunction, for example, the King, standing on a solar disc, holding out his hand to the Queen, who is standing on a crescent moon, all under the protection of a winged Mercury, or two riders riding against each other, a male figure on a sun-like animal, the lion, standing for sulphur, and a female, moon-like figure, riding on a gryphon (see figure 6). We can see the theme of union added to the theme of opposites in the symbols on their shields. The female's shield carries a sun, the male's shield a moon. In this basic way the dynamic aspect of the (chemical) change is suggested. The struggle of the two 'polarities' takes

Figure 6: The clash of opposites in the alchemical process: male and female, sulphur and mercury, engaged in knightly combat. On their shields each carries the symbol of the other. (From Stanislas Klossowski de Rola, *Alchemie*, Munich, Knaur Tb. Esoterik 4105, 1974.)

place for the sake of union — in 'chemical marriage'.

As far as our subject is concerned, it does not matter too much that the separate stages of the chemical reaction should be variously described. For there are common features: for example there are three (sometimes four) stages in the process. What they show, through colourful imagination, is a process of material-spiritual transformation.

In the first stage there is a condition of darkness (*nigredo*). This implies that there has already been a preliminary harmonization of chaotic elements. But soon Death (*mortificatio, putrefactio, calcinatio*) enters into this unified compound. This is what is meant by the picture of a black raven in these illustrations. The mystical experience recognizes a transitory phase of mystical death, in which 'old Adam with all his sins and evil lusts' dies — as in Martin Luther's *Little Catechism*. This transitory phase is *nigredo*.

C. G. Jung, in *Psychology and Alchemy*, describes the next stage in the process as follows:

Out of 'nigredo' comes a washing away (*ablutio, baptisma*) which leads directly to whiteness; or else the soul (*anima*), released by death, reunites with the dead body to a new life; or else many colours are transfused into one white colour which contains them all (*omnes*

colores, cauda payonis). By this means the first goal of the process is
reached, called *albedo, tinctura alba, terra alba foliata, lapis alba*, etc., a
stage glorified by some people as though the final goal had been
reached. However, this is only a silver (or moon) stage, which must
be transcended to reach a sun condition. The *albedo* is, so to speak,
twilight; but first there is *rubedo,* which is sunrise. Yellow (*citrinitas*)
describes the transition to *rubedo* which... later fades away. Then
by increasing the furnace to the highest degree, *rubedo* will unite
directly with *albedo.* So red and white are King and Queen, who also
in this final stage celebrate their *nuptiae chymicae* (chemical marriage).[4]

Symbolic parallels of this kind, thought to indicate a deeper
knowledge of nature, have been known for centuries, even
though there are not many descriptions which seem relevant
— though one occurs, for instance, in Part One of Goethe's
Faust. The young poet had ample opportunity to become
familiar with this field through tracts, treatises, and committed writings, and could pass it on in his own work.[5] Clearly
alluding to the alchemic union of opposites, Faust, during his
Easter walk with Wagner reports, as they reach the gate, how
his own father, 'A nobleman of sombre bearing', with other
adepts in an alchemist's laboratory, 'followed infinite recipes
to produce the fusion of the contrary [i.e. opposites]'. And elsewhere he says:

> A lion red there was who with a lily wedded
> In the warm pool; a suitor bold was he.
> Aflame were both, with naked fire urged on
> Repeatedly to seek their nuptial bed.
> The young queen, garbed in many hues,
> Appeared reflected in the glass.
> Here was the medicine. Yet the patients died,
> And no one questioned who survived.
> Our hellish potions in these vales and hills
> Worse havoc wrought than ever did the plague.

Certainly this is anything but a glorification of practices that
are scarcely understood any longer. Only the symbolism of the
lion and the lily, of flame and the nuptial bed, is still with us.
How far one was, or is, competent to decode this old mysterious language, is another story. At any rate it was a long time
before Jung, Herbert Silberer[6] and others found indications
that true alchemy did not take place only on a material plane.
Parecelsus raised the point that the *lumen naturae* (light of nature)
must be approached through *lumen gratiae* (light of grace). Only

a one-dimensional natural science or a healing method concerned with simple objects could make do with the 'light of nature' alone. We know Jakob Böhme and Angelus Silesius (Johann Scheffler) both made clear Christological references, and the *Philosophus Teutonicus*, who often used the vocabulary of alchemy alongside mystical-theological terminology, once advised:

Let it be clear to you seekers after the metallic tincture: if you would find the *lapidum philosophorum* (the Philosopher's Stone) then go and seek the rebirth of Christ.[7]

In other words, the chemical marriage referred to in alchemy corresponds to a new birth, the creation of a new person. Likewise the advice of Angelus Silesius:

Chemist, thy stone is nothing; the cornerstone, the one I mean, my gold tincture, is the Stone of all philosophers.[8]

Christian alchemists do not refer to the biblical image of a 'stone' by chance. For them the Philosopher's Stone (*lapis philosophorum*) is Christ himself. In fact we come across the lapis-Christus parallel in many connections. Jakob Böhme is by no means the last person whose intuitive thoughts revolved round the *mysterium magnum* and for whom all events took place on two planes, one heavenly, the other earthly — we could also say one mystical, the other chemo-cosmic. For as he once said: 'the heavenly shall turn the earthly into the heavenly, the eternal shall turn time into eternity.' Then Böhme goes on in a significant passage:

How strange to our minds that God ordained such an event as the *resurrection of man in Christ*, that He revealed Himself in such a pitiful and despised form in the flesh... as eternal birth is in him alone, so is the process of redemption after the Fall (sin), and so also is the process of the alchemists with their *lapidae philosophorum*. There is no difference between them, for all things stem from everlasting birth and all things must in some way be made whole.[9]

On the basis of the extensive material he accumulated in words and pictures, Jung follows, 'It is very clear from this material what alchemy was ultimately looking for: it wanted to create a *corpus subtile*, the transfigured resurrection of the body, i.e. a body that would be at the same time spirit...'[10]

How was this sublime result of alchemy visualized? The illustrations of alchemic treatises offer countless imaginative vari-

Figure 7: *Coniunctio* in an alchemical retort. (From Edward F. Edinger, *The Anatomy of the Psyche*, La Salle, Illinois, 1986.)

ations. First was the motif of male-female union: the two essences or tinctures as they united brought forth a child which itself bore the characteristics of them both, because the act was supposed to express wholeness. As Mercury represented the united essence of sun and moon, the fruit of chemical marriage was a hermaphrodite child, in the literal sense really a monstrous androgynous essence, sometimes also called *rebis* [thing] because in it were the signs of both poles, of sunshine and moonshine, of male and female. But neither the texts nor the diagrams and illustrations, often prepared with great care, were intended to be taken literally. For it really concerned a *trans-formation* of the masculine and the feminine and this was a spiritual event. The 'Philosopher's Stone' was no more to be taken literally as a stone than Christ was as the 'cornerstone' in the temple of the Christian community. Here, of course, what is of first importance is the restoration of the condition of wholeness in man. The alchemist, in his way, was trying to merge an existing duality into a single redemption-guaranteed unity, in the knowledge, however, that this mystery could only be prepared for; it was not available at will.

This sets a limit to what can be done outside the individual. True change begins within: from there light will shine on the whole world of human activity in the sense advised by the Paracelsian Gerhard Dorn (Dorneus):

Ex aliis numquam unum facies, quod quaeris, nisi prius ex te ipso fiat unum — You will never make the One you seek out of the Other, unless you first become *one* yourself![11]

In this way men, including those working with the tools of alchemy, are repeatedly thrown back on themselves. We are pointed in the same direction by, among others, Hildegard von Bingen (1098-1179) in her extensive scientific, cosmological and medical writing. Though she never used the word *Alchymia*, she did stress that mankind was the real *opus plenum*. The body and soul of man represent a *unum opus*. And Heinrich Schipperges, the research authority on Hildegard, adds by way of explanation: 'Man and wife are also seen in the anthropological sense as *opus alterum per alterum*, evoking the words ascribed to Hermes Trismegistos: "The work will be completed by both male and female."'[12] For *Ars totem requirit hominem* — everything to do with alchemy has as its aim *homo totus*, the whole man.

In the next chapter we shall discuss so-called chemical marriage against this traditional background, as presented by Johann Valentin Andreae at the beginning of the seventeenth century.

9

The Chemical Marriage of Christian Rosenkreutz

The double symbol of a cross and a rose conceals a mystery. It concerns the sect that today we call Rosicrucians, together with its competing organizations and brotherhoods, who chose this double symbol to represent the death of the 'old Adam' and a 'new life'. Johann Valentin Andreae,[1] a young Swabian theologian and pansophist of the early seventeenth century, summed up its meaning in a three-line mantra:

Ex deo nascimur
In Jesu morimur
Per spiritum reviviscimus
We are born of God
We die in Christ
We are born again through the Holy Ghost.

These words are in the closing section of Andreae's *Fama Fraternitatis*, with which he started a 'rumour' in 1614 that a Rosicrucian brotherhood had been formed. After a second publication entitled *Confessio Fraternitatis* (1615), his work, *Chymische Hochzeit Christiani Rosenkreutz anno 1459* [hereafter called *Chemical Marriage*], written earlier but printed in Strasbourg only in 1616, was circulated. It was this publication, which was interwoven with many enigmas, that took up the theme of mystical marriage and presented it in a highly symbolic and metaphorical way. It begins:

One evening before Easter Day I was sitting at the table. As usual I had uttered a humble prayer to my maker and had reflected on the many great mysteries which the Father of Light in his majesty had allowed me to observe fully. As I was thinking in my heart to prepare a pure, young chicken for my Easter Lamb, there came such a terrible, sudden wind that I thought the hillside where my dwelling was built would crumble under its great force. As the Devil, who has much troubled me, spared me this time, I took courage and continued my meditation until someone touched my back — something I was not expecting. This startled me so, I could scarcely bring myself to look round . . . there all dainty was the figure of a splendid, beautiful woman, her dress coloured blue with golden stars, like the sky.[2]

With this description the author introduced his 'chemical marriage' and presents Christian Rosenkreutz as a seeker after the spirit,[3] advanced in years, and living as a hermit. He describes his introspective, meditative manner on 'an evening before Easter Day'.

By giving this date he points to the central holy event of the Passion and Resurrection. And the pure Easter Lamb is to be understood as being prepared 'in my heart'. What he goes on to discuss also takes place *in the heart*.

We leave the level of everyday awareness for a scene of inner images (*imaginatio*) and inner perceptions (*inspiratio*) which develops during meditation. At the same time this is a prelude to an experience that takes place over 'seven days'. It can be compared to a dramatic mystery with seven acts, with the leading actor reporting on his experiences. To follow Alfons Rosenberg's interpretation: 'One much troubled, one racked by the power of his vision, has recorded in a state of shock the "great dream" of his longing, his eagerness, his striving, his impurity . . . one purpose of this mystic work was surely to draw out and strengthen mankind's higher powers.'[4]

In subsequent descriptions Christian Rosenkreutz, writing in the first person, reports his experiences on the way to the chemical marriage of a King and Queen. There are dangers, questions and doubts, temptations, fears and blessings. And as the drama unfolds with the image of 'that splendid, beautiful woman' dressed in blue, who visits the hermit with a special message, so in many individual scenes a similar spirit-form is introduced, whose role is to accompany the narrator and guide the course of the drama through a sign or a message. Like a *soror mystica* (mystical sister), found also among the alchemists, her task is to accompany the pilgrim on his journey — a journey that at the same time involves a special task. For whoever is given a personal letter by this woman has been singled out! He is invited to be a witness to take part in a wedding. The invitation has been signed by the *sponsus* and *sponsa* (bridegroom and bride) and it says:

Today, today, today
Is the King's wedding.
If you are born to this
Elected to joy by God
You are to climb the mountain,
Where three temples stand,
To see the event for yourself...

This thrice repeated 'today', presented almost as an incantation, makes it clear that the decision to take the spiritual path
to life's goal of *mysterium coniunctionis* brooks no delay. *Now* is
the time for decision and *you yourself* must resolve upon it! Now
is the time to risk an inner ascent to the 'three temples'. From
ancient times, has not the mountain been the place where gods
meet, the place of *Hieros Gamos*? That is where the event is to
be observed, i.e. the inner experience to be realized. Meditative study offers the possibility of inner fulfilment scarcely less
important for alchemists than for mystics. Those adept in the
art of alchemy taught their pupils not to put aside books they
had read once, twice or three times, but to go on reading them
until they became so permeated and coloured by them as to
be led to a spontaneous inner experience. The wedding invitation continues:

Are you being watchful?
Look to yourself!
Bathe yourself diligently
Lest the marriage bring you harm
Harm may befall whoever hesitates
Let him beware who is too lightweight!

The pilgrims to the shrine knew too that only those who had
purified themselves should attempt to climb the holy mountain. The basic requirement for the first stage of the inner
spiritual path was catharsis (cleansing). The marriage would
bring harm to whoever set out unclean, impure or unprepared.

Watchfulness, self-study and self-knowledge were the essential requirements for a genuine mystic as for an alchemist. Over
the entrance to 'chemical marriage' was written: *Gnothi seau-
ton* (Know thyself!), the same words the ancient Greeks had
written over the entrance to their temple courtyards. 'Bathe
yourself diligently' here means spare no effort in preparation.
Here too belongs the warning the writer gives in describing
the seven-day experience; a warning that on the great day of

reckoning one could be found 'too lightweight'. Again the right moment plays a decisive role: 'Harm may befall whoever hesitates' and so loses the never-to-be-repeated moment of decision. In the spiritual life *Kairos* [opportunity] reigns, not *Chronos*, i.e. not measured, quantitative time, but time in the sense of the right moment. And this decisive here-and-now is part of every serious spiritual exercise such as prayer, meditation and taking part in a sacramental service in the presence of the Holy Spirit. A proper concentration of the soul will arise spontaneously from this resolve, and above all a responsive surrender of the innermost being. Any conscious effort of will to reach this state would be inappropriate.

Regarding preparation, it is worth noting that those invited to the marriage of the king and queen will put on special garments. We recall the verses of the New Testament about the 'proper' wedding garment (Matthew 22:11-12). Christian Rosenkreutz put on a white linen robe and girded his loins with a red sash fixed over his shoulders crosswise. This is the origin of the shape of the cross of St Andrew. In addition he put four red roses in his hat before he set out on his pilgrimage. It is obvious that the author is speaking of himself and his own spiritual experience, for the Andreae family had in its coat-of-arms a St Andrew's cross with four roses! But this is only a partial explanation because there is more basic symbolism: the polarity

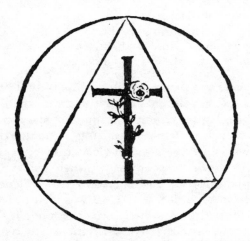

Figure 8: The union of cross and rose. An expression of death and new life. (From *Die Bruderschaft der Rosenkreuz*, ed. Gerhard Wehr, Cologne, 1984, Diederich's Gelbe Reihe [Yellow Series] 53.)

of white and red and the union of cross and rose as they express death and new life. Again these elements are united in the person and name of Christian Rosenkreutz. Such a name commits one; it immediately sets a programme for life for any active Christian who follows the true Christ, that is through his Crucifixion and Resurrection. The fact that no roses bloom at Easter should no more give us pause than a number of other inconsistencies that appear in the text of *Chemical Marriage*. The reader should be clear that this is a description beyond references and incidents, that the boundary of reality has been crossed — just as in dreams or fairy stories. What may seem real on the face of it refers to spiritual matters and processes.

The author of *Chemical Marriage* is in any case not the fictitious, though at the same time archetypal, Christian Rosenkreutz. He is simply a satire on contemporary alchemy, which had by that time fallen into decadence—as is the whole work according to some critics. Earlier in this chapter we discussed a kind of journey of the spirit. Admittedly it was a special sort of journey, for it was not the way of the mystic nor yet the classical inner way. Why?

The difference is that alchemy thrives on the 'powers of nature', of which Jakob Böhme wrote in his *Aurora* that they should be 'assiduously taken into account', and included in the process of understanding and maturing through which the 'seeker' has to travel. Here there is no isolated contemplation of the soul, rejecting the natural world. The sixteenth- and seventeenth-century Pansophists, emulating the great Paracelsus, held the same view, paying attention to signs that would speak to all the senses, acting as 'receptacles of the spirit' (Jakob Böhme) and which could be regarded as living proof of the divine word. As Rudolf Steiner put it in his fundamental article on Andreae's book, in which he points out how mysticism and alchemy differ:

The research of mystics and alchemists lie in opposite directions. The mystic goes straight to the individual spiritual heart of man. His goal (which can be regarded as *mystical marriage*) is the union of the conscious mind with its own spiritual essence. The alchemist, however, aims to traverse the spiritual territory of nature so that at the end of the journey, by virtue of the knowledge acquired during it, he can perceive the spiritual essence of man. His goal is *chemical marriage*, union with the spiritual territory of nature. Only after this union will he be able to perceive the essence of mankind.[5]

Thus two basic attitudes can be clearly identified even if it has to be conceded that (as we have seen) a mystical-meditative element does have a place in Christian Rosenkreutz's alchemy. Turning inwards (introversion) and turning outwards (extraversion) are not always to be met with in pure form, though they are both known psychological types (according to analytical psychology). For whoever pursues a qualitative scientific search and strives for knowledge of the world, which is the alchemist's first aim, will not do so without *self*-knowledge. This is shown clearly in the introduction to Andreae's *Chemical Marriage*.

Both basic attitudes are related to each other and can be seen as functions of one another. Both attitudes can be compared with each other, and above all they both introduce a *coniunctio* in which first one then the other tends to go to extremes. One thinks of the relationship between the macrocosmic world and the microcosmic human being, and how an almost endless range of experience extends between what is 'above' and what is 'below'. Here the natural philosophers of the ancient world as well as of the Middle Ages can be eloquent teachers. In this mobile field things 'happen' that hold the world together at its centre. The task of the Rosicrucian alchemists was to penetrate the secret roots of man and the world, and to alter matter, first changing oneself. Hence the stern injunction already referred to, of the Paracelsian doctor, Gerhard Dorn (Dorneus): '*Transmutemini in vivos lapides philosophicos* — Transmute yourselves into living Philosophers' Stones!' The *Chemical Marriage* of Christian Rosenkreutz, the model image of true alchemy, not to be confused with the mercenary pursuit of transmuting base metal to gold, embraces nature, including man, in a spiritual process of change. Self-knowledge is extended by knowledge of the world, while knowledge of the world is deepened by self-knowledge.

Let us now continue to follow the path of our pilgrim — a path which started in a hermit's cell, the cell of one who meditates. This cell is at the same time a symbolic expression of an introverted state of mind. However, all this changes, for he follows a path which leads into a forest and through the world where there are many false trails and much strife. Worldly knowledge was an important part of the Rosicrucian approach, for it was a key point for the Rosicrucian, as for Christians in general, not to flee from the world but to face it, indeed to change it.

A biographical factor comes into play here to be mentioned in passing. Johann Valentin Andreae himself travelled widely. But as he did not write a realistic biography in the generally accepted sense, we cannot expect his mystery-drama to contain realistic descriptions. Much of what he reports bears a more generalized stamp and is coloured by symbolism and allegory. As in our own experience of dreams, the imaginative element overwhelmingly predominates.

To describe briefly the further stages of the 'seven days', Christian Rosenkreutz reaches the castle he is seeking and gains admittance. Together with many others, mostly unworthy 'seekers', he has to undergo a series of trials. Accompanied by many puzzles and mysteries, the wedding of the royal couple draws ever nearer.

Despite the tortuous, baroque language of *Chemical Marriage*, the text is clear enough to convey its meaning either in metaphor or between the lines. Other contemporary fellow-pilgrims are on their way to the wedding on the mystical-chemical path, yet their ability to gain understanding is inadequate and out-of-date. We hear of examples of human delusion that, as the author describes, must be judged and drastically punished. There are, for example, the pseudo-alchemists, the so-called gold-transmuters, and the 'bunglers' who are lacking in spiritual resources and in dedication to the spiritual goal. The author of the *Marriage* bears in mind throughout those who follow the maxim: '*Aurum nostrum non est aurum vulgi* — our gold is no ordinary gold!'

In this respect Andreae clearly showed his point of view by distancing himself from any unworthy contemporaries who brought such discredit on the true esoteric faith.

Many imaginary scenes are described in *Chemical Marriage*, interspersed with dream images and allegories. There is, for example, a scene with a 'beautiful snow-white unicorn'. Of this he says: 'It ran to a stream and knelt down on its forelegs in order to pay homage to a lion which was standing so motionless in the stream that it might have been made of stone or metal.'

Unicorn and lion stand in relation to each other as head to heart. Both of these should be brought into harmony at this important moment in the development of spiritual awareness, that is, when they exhibit a human dimension, arrived at either as an expression of an analytical critical mind, or through the techniques of quantitative, experimental natural science. Harmonization of the powers of head and heart, otherwise of thought and feeling, needs to be attempted in order to avoid a self-sufficient rationalism or an amoral natural science aiming merely at the practical and functional. The opposition of lion and unicorn is to be understood as an allegorical depiction at a time when the science of the early seventeenth century and the emancipating power of thought tended towards a one-sided rationalism. It is not difficult either to realize from this, in what dilemma we find ourselves today, when there has obviously been failure to carry out *coniunctio* between head and heart.

This succession of images drawn as though from the personal experiences of Christian Rosenkreutz subsequently takes on more and more the character of an alchemic transmutation process. A strange drama is staged that describes in seven acts the seven steps for penetrating the Great Mystery. So before the royal marriage can be followed to its culmination, Christian Rosenkreutz has to undergo one last ordeal. He has to witness the decapitation of the entire royal family. Great is his horror and distress. One more effort is then required of him, viz. 'to spare no effort in helping to bring the buried King back to life'. In alchemical terms it is the transition from *nigredo* (blackness) to *albedo* (whiteness). We are reminded of the theme of resurrection.

The result of all this suffering is a special kind of vision. A wonderful bird, the phoenix, arises — symbolizing transformation, resurrection, the renewal of life from the ashes, and hence basically a process of cremation that must be gone through. The egg of the phoenix is cut open with a diamond and the blood of the mysterious bird finally brings about the awakening of the dead.

Yet there is no new life without sacrifices, without the shedding of life-blood! Astonishingly, those raised from the dead first take the form of 4-inch-tall homunculi; they look like a dwarf man and a dwarf woman. These two agree to marry. The wedding takes place straightaway, behind a curtain, watched over by Cupid, the attendant of Venus.

The ceremony of the wedding, which the book makes clear is to be consummated *within* man as a *mysterium coniunctionis*, transforms the successful alchemists, themselves purified through the role of being participants and witnesses of the marriage, into 'Knights of the Golden Stone'. From now on a duty is laid on them to protect the true art of transmutation — the transforming agent is associated with self-completion — as servants of the natural order (*ars naturae ministra*). Christian Rosenkreutz accepts the same duty as a Knight of the Golden Stone. In this way, on the seventh day, he achieves the goal of his pilgrimage.

However, a bitter drop of wormwood mars the happy mood of the new initiate, for being guilty of an unpardonable offence, he is assigned to be guard of the outer gate. While going through the mysterious castle in the company of his servant, he had ventured right into the innermost courtyard and into the inner sanctum. There he did not stop outside the bedchamber of Venus and uncovered the naked beauty of her body — a forbidden sight!

The biographer of J. V. Andreae observes that as a young student Andreae was once sent down from the High School in Tübingen on account of an incident similar to this. It is not said what youthful *faux pas* he committed. We shall not be far wrong, however, in regarding this somewhat obscure episode as related to the allegory and giving a biographical meaning to it, and in seeing it as a basic problem in the process of initiation or growing up. Most important to be considered here is the inner struggle within the soul (*anima* or *animus*) which, according to Jung, plays a decisive role in the process of initiation or individuation.

Shortly before the end, our Rosicrucian narrative breaks off suddenly in mid-sentence. This is followed by a puzzling note that 'two quarto sheets' are missing. The fragmentary character of the *Chemical Marriage* is surely more than a literary device. For Andreae's long account is so dramatically told that it must spring from an impulse to relate his *own* inner experience. It is *this* which gives the text its esoteric nature. And its incompleteness may perhaps underline how very 'open' it is, open for the reader and any spectator who will let the images and scenes speak to him.

Besides, this is not the only esoteric writing that is fragmentary and *must* remain so. Barely four years before the publication of Andreae's *Chemical Marriage*, Jakob Böhme left unfinished 'as though broken off in a storm' his famous first work, *Aurora or The Rising Sun* (1612). Or take the no less famous fragments of Novalis, who in his own way was party to the mystery of mystical marriage. In this case as in the others, even fragments of this kind can act as spiritual seeds. Munich's congenial Romantic, Franz von Baader, speaks specifically of *fermenta cognitionis*, i.e. of a force driving the individual along the path to understanding and maturity.[6] In any case it is enough that the direction and separate stages of the Way are recorded. Writing about a mystery cannot do more. It is left to the free will of each individual to do what is necessary to put himself on the path and (as in the closing remarks of *Chemical Marriage*) finally 'to come home'. So seen, Christian Rosenkreutz is a prototype and human ideal always capable of realization anew and permitting no imitation.

It must be mentioned that the mystery of chemical marriage, with it mysterious *coniunctio*, also runs through Goethe's *Faust*. The poet tells Charlotte von Stein in a letter dated June 1787, that he has 'read right through a beautiful fairy-tale — viz. Andreae's *Chemical Marriage of Christian Rosenkreutz*'. Jung, who had a copy of Part Two of *Faust* with him all his life, confessed it was first through reading Andreae's work 'that he began to see daylight'; 'and it was only the study of classical and early medieval works that convinced me that *Faust*, Parts One and Two, represent an *opus alchymicum* in the best sense.' The mystery of *coniunctio*, of chemical marriage, runs through the poet's entire two-part work.[7] Even psychoanalysis can be traced back to the 'numinous influence' that radiates, backwards as well as forwards, from Goethe's chief work.

'Christ and Sophie': The *Mysterium Coniunctionis* in the Work of Novalis

The precocious poet, Friedrich von Hardenberg, known as Novalis, used the theme of *mysterium coniunctionis* thoughtfully and lyrically in his work as no other poet did. Indeed from the beginning the young philosopher's poetic fantasy and power of reflection revolved round the focus of love that was revealed yet hidden, the wedding of King and Queen, and the idea of marriage as a physical-mental-spiritual mystery. But his works take their existential-numinous character from his own experience of love, in his early relationship with his sweetheart Sophie. The youthful versifier was to become a poet, the apprentice was to become the Magus of the Romantics, the great Christian esoteric. For the theme that was to run through his work was: 'We do not know the depths of our spirit. The mysterious path is an inward one.'[1] This inner path, which Novalis travelled all his life, is not simply to be equated with a subjectively dominated contemplative nature. His introspection, his looking inward, is never self-enclosed or isolated. As 'one endowed with sensibility', he has to reveal his feelings so that others can be made aware of the fullness of life. What is hidden in a state of mystery becomes visible. This is how he puts it in one of his 'Sacred Songs' about Christ—which are, by the way, purely in keeping with Böhme in spirit and inspiration:

> He is the star, he the sun's course
> Of life eternal he the source
> From plant and stone, from light and sea
> His pure presence shines on me.

The material and the transcendental are -- as with Jakob Böhme — no longer separated from each other. They are closely connected. They permeate one another. The fruit of this amalgamation is a 'holy open secret', as Goethe put it, now and in the future.

For Friedrich von Hardenberg the decisive turning point on the path to an inner life with his meeting with Sophie von Kühn. His relationship with this adolescent girl is certainly open to different interpretations — depending on one's point of view and attitude. Here we shall deal briefly only with the aspect the poet considered critical for his own life, viz., as an initiation into the mysteries of love and death. 'A quarter of an hour settled it for me,' he admitted to his brother Erasmus, when he told him about their first meeting. In the sense of the esoteric tradition we can speak here about *mysterium coniunctionis*. For in his love affair with this young girl Novalis had found his true Ego — in psychological terms — his Self.

The encounter can be quickly outlined. Seen from the outside 'nothing special' happened: a young man suddenly became aware that he had met not one of many possible loves but the One, the Beloved. And although Eros spoke his unmistakable, passionate, hot-blooded language, of which Novalis has furnished many explicit examples, he clearly felt that 'there are closer relationships than those that blood unites'. Where more is involved than a short-lived sentimental surge of feelings, then a different kind of standard is required. The feelings must endure even in the presence of death. Only when Sophie died from tuberculosis after much suffering, and only when the days of sorrow for those made lonely were over, did the light of a new life, so to speak, begin to shine through for her lover from the *other* side of reality. Only then did the betrothed couple appear to be joined in a mystical marriage.

Though Novalis might say while his bride was alive that she bore the same name as the subject he was studying, i.e. 'philosophy', yet the true transcendent experience came to him only *after* Sophie's death. Only then had he become aware in the full meaning of the words, of a spiritual reality — which before he had known about, reflected upon and circled round in a poetic manner. But it was only then that this reality appeared bound up with the name and person of this one human being. Now the eyes of the spirit, the perceptive organs of a higher order, were opened. One might ask the question: was the image of the soul revealed to Novalis no more than an image of Sophie von Kühn's memory, her individual character, including bad habits; or had a much greater and totally different dimension entered his life?

What is remarkable here in the history of Christianity undoubtedly lies in the fact that Friedrich von Hardenberg, brought up as a deeply pious Protestant, found a way through his experience of love and death to reach the reality of the divine Sophia. In this way he broke through a narrow, one-sided and patriarchally-orientated piety and theology, just as Jakob Böhme had done. The archetypal image of the divine Sophia came again on to the horizon of individual experience, as we have seen it do in the late-Jewish books of wisdom, in gnosticism, in the mystics (*sapientia*), and not least in the school of Jakob Böhme. Novalis could only tell himself that he had not lost Sophie's essential spiritual form. In reality he had only then really found her, the hitherto unknown side of his own creative Self. Meeting on Earth was only a prelude, and her physical death was not an end but a beginning, an initiation for meeting on a new level of being. Novalis himself has left us plenty of examples to support this.

On one occasion he describes a vision he saw when he visited the grave of his dead bride. When he was 25 years old he noted in his diary, on 13 May 1797:

In the evening I went to Sophie. I was indescribably happy there — a moment radiant with rapture. I blew away the grave like dust before me. Centuries were like moments — I could feel her presence — I thought she was about to step forward.

From that vision by the graveside and that reported in 'Hymns to the Night' there dates the poetry of the Novalis we know, not only the poet of the 'blue flower' of the Romantics, but that of a man haunted by inner experience, initiated into the mysteries of the night and the marriage of the dead. At the same time let us not underestimate what an important role his second bride, Julie von Charpentier, played in his later work, that is, during the rest of his short life until his death on 25 March 1801. Nor was his second love relationship at all a contradiction of his unique love for Sophie von Kühn. Rather this 'last love', as he once called it in a poem, presupposed as a prerequisite his transcendent experience with Sophie, raising the human encounter to a higher level.

It is a fact that in his songs and hymns Novalis was able to make Eros once again a cult figure without abandoning a spiritual interpretation of things. After nearly 2,000 years during which love, the erotic and sex were regarded with suspicion, devalued and thought to be the Devil's work, they now deserved to be given due honour — not least in our time, when they are threatened, almost from the opposite pole, by gross sexuality and renewed false values.

This Eros, whose imagery Novalis stretches to include the transubstantiation of flesh and blood, and who encompasses the entire natural world, can be compared with a soaring archway spanning the divided current of fate and so holding out the prospect of *unio mystica*. This arch is thrown poetically and intellectually across the gulf between matter and spirit, in this world and the next, by one of whom it can be said that he has 'guessed the high meaning of the earthly body'. For, as it says in the hymn celebrating physical love and the Last Supper combined in a single whole:

> Few know
> Love's secret
> Feel its endless hunger
> And eternal thirst.
> The divine meaning
> Of the Last Supper
> Puzzles earthly minds;
> But whoso once
> Drew breath of life
> From warm, beloved lips,
> Whose heart did melt
> O'ercome by quiv'ring waves
> Of fire divine,
> Whose eye was raised
> To gauge heav'n's endless depths
> This man will eat
> His body, drink His blood,
> For all eternity...

Here speaks a visionary, because his 'eyes were raised'. Now he takes in, as it were at a glance, the whole future of mankind, as he continues elsewhere (but still in the same intellectual-symbolic setting):

> The eternal Kingdom has been founded
> In love and peace all conflict ends
> The long nightmare of pain is over,
> Sophie, ever the heart's priestess.

These lines close the first part of an unfinished novel, *Heinrich von Ofterdingen*, called 'Expectation'. We should recall here other verses, full of foreboding, written while Sophie was still alive, in which the poet anticipates with remarkable clear-sightedness later elements of his vision:

> . . .
> Must I be bereft for ever then? Is surmise
> Of union in time to come the same
> As that we knew already as our own,
> But yet not quite possessed?
> . . .
> Thou art not in thy cups — thou voice of genius,
> Our immortality thou dost perceive,
> And conscious art thou of that very value,
> Disclosed here to us only one by one.
> One day mankind will be in grace
> Perfect as Sophie to me now.
> Then will its higher consciousness
> Be no more changed with haze of wine.

The linked phrase from the diary that Novalis kept in the days following Sophie's death, and which can be taken as the key to his whole spiritual-religious understanding is:

Christ and Sophie.

With this, Novalis left far behind him the position of the traditional church which was fixed by dogma and denominational formulae. He pushed open the door to a Christianity that put mankind on a path — individually as well as in a cosmic sense — which could be followed to a *coniunctio*. Novalis had experienced this in anticipation, a binding together of flesh and spirit, earth and heaven. The metaphor of physical love and the Last Supper serves to bring mystical marriage back into the area of individual experience. It is significant that both material and sacramental dimensions are included. One can speak therefore of a double aspect in the Christian esoteric just as we encounter it on the one hand in mysticism and on the other in alchemy and the origins of Rosicrucianism.[2] It includes both self-knowledge and knowledge of the world; mystical and chemical marriage together.

Martin Beheim-Schwartzbach said of Novalis that he was 'an esoteric in the deepest sense, according to St John's definition, for whom no physical distance and no remoteness of mystery was beyond reach and who associated with mystics as an equal,'³ and Friedrich Hiebel, summing up in his biography of Novalis, made this judgement:

With him a new era of Christian existence began, based on knowledge of the pure Ego. He set before us a type of Christian discipleship that never existed before. His longing to return to a Golden Age sprang from his wholehearted readiness to become childlike in St John's sense of becoming a child before God. Even people who in his time knew him only from afar, sensed this. . . In Novalis, arising within him in visionary moments, there lived a feeling that the time was coming when Christ's presence was assured. Only gradually has he become recognized in our century. As a man of the future he will go on into the next millennium. His influence is growing worldwide. His word of the nearness of Christ will continue.⁴

The interpreter's words have themselves become prophetic. How will they be fulfilled? It is undeniable that in the text and images of Von Hardenberg there is an inner power to fascinate, from which one can escape only with difficulty. It is a fascination suffused with divinity not least because the *mysterium coniunctionis* is solemnly promised. Thus earth-bound mortals can also immediately share in the love of Friedrich and Sophie. In his own words Novalis says:

The great mystery is open to all while it remains for ever unfathomable. A new world will be born from pain and our mortal dust dissolved in tears in the cup of eternal life. In each one dwells a heavenly mother to bear each child for ever. Do you not feel the sweet birth in the heartbeat within your breast?

11

Mystical Marriage in Modern Times: A Report

It is characteristic of our times that more and more people hanker after deep intellectual-spiritual and religious experience. Interest in what is written in this field has increased to an astonishing degree. The question is: what is the state of modern spiritual understanding? Should spiritual vision or psychic perception belong only to a long-vanished past, something in which one had just 'kept up' an interest?

It needs no special debate to know that this is incorrect. There is plenty of evidence. The problem is rather: how is what belongs inside oneself — intellectual-spiritual vision or what is seen as an extraordinary phenomenon — to be reconciled with today's state of knowledge? Must we opt out intellectually and spiritually, as many advise? Must we cast our minds back to long out-of-date (atavistic) states of knowledge and damp down our active Ego-awareness, in order to reach the sources of spirituality? Or is there a legitimate way, i.e. an appropriate spiritual as well as modern way to the transcendental?

Of course advocates of one or another modern 'spiritual science' will say that this last-mentioned option is possible. We need only to follow the instructions of our teacher. Well and good. But there are two alternatives: either to follow a path of learning which results eventually in 'knowing', and in having one's teacher's words off by rote, or to take part in a living experience. But what about the authenticity and credibility of this kind of experience?

Instead of putting forward a catalogue of tests of authenticity, I shall report here on the experience of a woman of our day, which may be said to be a perfect example in many respects. The phenomenon as such — 'automatic writing' — has been experienced by countless people, both past and present. But what is remarkable in this case is the way the woman learned to harness her gift, the expansion of consciousness she enjoyed and how she was able to use her experience as a way towards maturity.

The person in question is Irmengard Bardo, who was born in 1909. Behind this pseudonym lies hidden a woman, who as a wife, housewife, mother of two children, and not least as a creative artist, never felt the need to publicize what had happened to her.[1] The facts vouch for her need to remain unknown, for she admitted to her automatic writing only in 1946. In the years since then Frau Bardo has collected an impressive quantity of carefully documented material.[2] But first we need a short introduction.

To help a friend disturbed about the fate of her husband, who was reported missing in the war, Irmengard Bardo accompanied her to a medium. This was in a village in Upper Bavaria. Neither of the young women believed in the 'hocus pocus' of the proceedings. The medium used a small board, with the help of which, writing dictated from 'beyond' sometimes materialized. (The pencil moved involuntarily in the medium's hand, hurried from letter to letter and 'wrote'.) Only the distressing uncertainty caused by the internal and external strains of the post-war period explains why anyone should consult such a village oracle.

'We could do that too,' the two women thought, and to this end one of them tried with a board like the medium's, on which the alphabet was written out, but without success. Either her hand, which was supposed to write automatically, did not move, or she helped it along and nothing came of it. This first attempt, which was not taken seriously, broke up in laughter. But that same evening, as Irmengard was sitting alone in her room, she took it into her head to try again. She herself reports what happened:

At first my hand lay quite still for some time; I had closed my eyes. Nothing stirred. By this time I thought I couldn't do it at all. Then suddenly my hand literally moved about! It drew big circles; it went over the paper several times in large curves until it stopped. I saw the letters through half-open eyes. The event was so shattering that it affected my whole body. It was like a compulsive rhythmic movement, being involved in something I couldn't stop and that was more or less involuntary.[3]

Irmengard opened her eyes and put together the letters that

had been picked out. She was greatly astonished, for in fact a text had appeared. True, the content and form was strange and new and a clear meaning was not expressed. But there were words which fascinated the writer: 'You gift day... Flowers — colour — light... Rainbow — morning — seed, the stars... Flame under ravens... Whatever [happens] don't be afraid!'

Who was the author of this word puzzle, and to what mysterious association did it point? 'It could not have come from me personally,' she reported confidently. 'Besides, I was almost in a trance while it was being written. I was completely confused by the outcome. I studied the text over and over again; I could not fathom where it had come from and I also felt it was rather sinister. But I still felt drawn to the page with the text on it, as if by magic.'

As we are not discussing automatic writing here as such, we shall break off. For what started in the mediumistic circumstances reported above took on new forms in course of time. Above all, it began to throw light on the conscious mind. And as Irmengard Bardo could not tell anyone else about the inner impulse which caused this spontaneous writing phenomenon, she started to study the contents herself. A strange sequence of event ensued, in accordance with a process of intellectual-spiritual maturing. The significance of this is obvious when one looks back over the more than three decades that have passed since the event itself. A turning-point occurred when one day — 25 February 1946 — an almost uncoded message was received, bearing the signature 'Lot'.

Now I was speechless... In large clear letters on the page was the name [Lot]. That was the character from the Old Testament I had never thought of in the least, and now here he was disturbing my thoughts and feelings. To begin with I just stared at this name, then I saw it indistinctly, as though through a haze, for tears were pouring uncontrollably from my eyes. 'Lot' — I shivered. How was it that this patriarch from the Bible turned to me of all people? I tried slowly to take all this in. It was impossible. Only a feeling of respect and humility overcame me.

After this the writer first had the idea of a spiritual identity existing *outside* her own psyche. What was important at this juncture was, that with the emergence of Lot, the possibility arose of a complete personal analysis. The message received was partly in verse, with simple, unsophisticated rhymes. The receiver could refer questions back and, writing automatically, obtain the required answers. There is a close comparison with the 'active imagination' of Jung. This is a psychotherapeutic procedure of discussion with the unconscious, in which the receiver of internally created images conducts a dialogue with them and allows himself to receive an answer which again arises out of the unconscious. Frau Bardo then, and for many years after, had no knowledge of psychoanalysis. That applies also to the religious or mystical-historical themes in the texts which were written automatically or intuitively. That she was involved in something with these kinds of connections, reminiscent of mystical experiences, did not occur to her, because she knew nothing of such matters. It seemed at the time to be a spontaneous experience for which the writer for years could find no possible explanation. But even if she looked on Lot as an historical person, she still nevertheless felt an inner bond with him:

I felt him coming from 'above', from 'on high', from 'Heaven'. . . So I lived inwardly closely bound up with Lot and kept myself ready for his communications at every quiet moment I was free. My devout belief, which affected my whole being, led me to do what I was asked by Lot, my guide.

This readiness went so far that Frau Bardo accepted 'without question' the information that she should now die, as a sacrifice for her son:

The order was that at the hour of my death, which was to be at 9 p.m., I should go from this earth singing and with a joyful expression. I took this command to die literally. . . I waited for approaching death, which didn't seem frightening, but which would take me to a light, free kingdom, to the spiritual leader I knew. But nothing happened.

The writer did not know that there is such a thing as 'mystical death';[4] and she knew even less of the possibility of mystical marriage. Yet it was marriage which Lot announced to her in the messages that followed.

The record continues: 'I took this communication literally too. I did not reflect on it but simply did everything I was told to do.' As she says in her own writing, as well as in the 'writing from the medium', what occurred seemed too overpowering. While the so-called death had passed without particular incident, that is without any dramatic break with the 'Old

Adam', this time, as the bride of Lot, it was impressed on her that she had to be 'quite pure within', that her day of purification was at hand and she had to fast. That is what she did:

I scarcely slept, for I wrote down, whenever it was possible, everything I was told. Many songs, verses and conversations come from those days. I felt the bond with Lot as a reality that I fully experienced. I felt so safe at this time and I was always suffused with such a feeling of happiness that I cannot put it into words. I no longer understood how it was that I used often to feel anxious and uncertain about life. Now I was lifted up and protected in a world that, although it was invisible to my eyes, had more reality and power for my feelings than the world of our five senses.

Irmengard reported further how in her 'days of purification' she had to wage an inner battle, a conflict between God and the Devil. She thought she heard 'loud voices' and (in mid-February) rolling thunder. A cautious check on her surroundings told her that these noises originated in 'her own perception'. 'Also I could feel no firm ground under my feet. The earth shook continually and I heard frightening rumblings coming from its depths. . . within me the battle between the powers of light and darkness was developing.' The writer thought that everything at that time was to be traced back to the influence of a 'spirit world'. We shall now quote in full that part of the report that has a bearing on the *mysterium coniunctio*:

I also believed in the forthcoming marriage ceremony with Lot and was prepared for this great event on the evening of 27 February, when everyone was in bed and the house was quiet. I sensed Lot near me, knew that today I was to celebrate marriage with him, and surrendered to the rising emotions that filled me. In all humility and gratitude, intent on what was happening, I wanted to be filled with the spiritual light that inclined towards me, full of grace. Lot and I were very near one another; I felt this strongly as I wrote down the conversation that developed between us. Its words sounded like a devout antiphony and stirred my soul to its depths. It swelled in a rhythm almost like a litany, which through constant repetition of suppliant invocations, moved my feelings and like magic lifted my spirit. I believed myself translated to another world, a spirit world, and that I was fully part of it.

At this moment of greatest happiness, feeling spiritually one, I saw coming from the centre of my body, above the navel, a white cloud-like mass [known in parapsychology as the phenomenon of ectoplasm] which condensed into a ghostly essence. It suggested a figure no more than some 2ft (60cm) which floated to the window and disappeared through it. The room seemed to grow unlimited in size...

Soon after this climax, the writing with which I had quickly filled several pages became more untidy and eventually quite unreadable. Despite all efforts I could not decipher the conclusion. Moreover, after the departure of the vaporous mass I could remember nothing. I know only that I woke up next morning on a couch, fully dressed, feeling ill, and with a violent headache centred at the top of my head. I had to overcome this temporary indisposition to see to my son, as I did every day before he went to school.

When Christian had left the house I lay down again for a while, for I felt very tired. I lay so that I could see the window. The sun was shining in. Its rays reached me across the room and dazzled me. I could not help looking into its light as though spellbound and suddenly saw a vision. Moving towards me I saw something like a wide, undulating beam of green light, dark at the edges, coming straight out of the sun. The orb of the sun, however, was wrapped in the most wonderful soft colours of the rainbow. In this sea of colour surrounding the sun was a strip of writing in Gothic lettering. At the same time I heard wondrous sounds of unearthly beauty. It was as though the whole heavenly host had broken into a great song of joy. This vision soon vanished. At the same time I felt light as air, and would not have been surprised if I had floated off the ground. Now the bands of Gothic writing appeared in the room (I could not make sense of it), covering the walls and all the furniture. As I was weak from fasting and my headache had come back, I became anxious. But my fears went away when I took my notepad and wrote. The message I received filled many pages written very legibly all in Gothic script (for the wedding ceremony with Lot the writing had been mainly in Roman), which moved me very deeply because of what they said.

So much for Irmengard Bardo's report of her experience. It goes without saying that it needs a commentary which on the one hand would take into account the broad context of this woman's whole history, and on the other would draw on the many allusions and parallels in religious and spiritual history to explain it — in particular the experience of Christian mystics (for example, the green or viridian vision of Hildegard von Bingen) as well as Eastern esoterics. In view of our theme, however, we need only make the few following points.

It is worth noting first that when she experienced this death and marriage Frau Bardo had reached middle age; in 1946 she was 37 years old. Lot, the commanding, guiding form she talked to, corresponded to an authority superior to the everyday Ego and indeed was experienced as a religio-numinous essence; hence her unquestioning submission. It is noteworthy too that the occurrences were not accepted passively. What took place was more a discussion in which the Ego became a partner in dialogue and communication even with this superior authority. As a result a widening of consciousness was achieved which was limited by the extent to which the Ego-consciousness had grown sufficiently to be able to experience the 'other side', followed by relapse into the sleep of the unconscious. It is not just the metaphor of marriage that is the crucial factor in this process, but the communicative event itself that is the meeting of the Ego with an Ego-transcending psychic dimension. C. G. Jung speaks of the Self in this connection and we shall consider this separately. The very gradual nature of self-realization can be seen clearly in the fact that Irmengard Bardo took over 30 years to achieve it; her later texts, written consciously but still automatically (that is, basic statements made without the Ego in control) show equally this maturing process. In this woman the Ego and the Self do come together literally and exactly in full correspondence. And in her special case a union takes place on an emotional level, in which the inner guide of her soul (Lot) describes her as 'participating with him in the marriage ceremony'. It is worth noting that the announcements of 'death' and 'marriage', at first taken literally by Frau Bardo, can very well be 'understood' and integrated, according to their symbolic content, as enriching her life and making it whole.

Finally, it may seem that this individual example of *coniunctio* is a long way removed from the religio-mythic-historic evidence of mystical marriage reported at the beginning. However, though Irmengard Bardo's experience may have taken place as a result of automatic writing, yet it is coloured above all by the Christian bride-mystery known since Böhme and Novalis. The phenomenon of automatic or intuitive writing is thus of secondary importance. It merely plays the role of a vehicle, though it is 'writing from within' and not an external stunt. The spellbinding, numinous nature of the experience is beyond doubt and it is clear that through it Frau Bardo found fulfilment. She herself sums up her experience in a first, and until now exclusive newspaper article:

My consciousness was enlarged and broadened, through looking deeply into my soul, exploring its secrets, bringing them into consciousness and living with them in one whole — that is, I kept the material and the transcendent in a healthy balance. My experience was quite different from the usual run of 'spiritualism' which often creates a dubious atmosphere round the 'medium'. For this reason many people focus on the fascination of an event bordering on the miraculous, and not on the spiritual power which is hidden in us all, and can be activated in some people so as to shower themselves and others with beneficial help.[5]

12

Towards Self-Realization through Psychoanalysis.

So far we have seen how the theme of mystical marriage and the image of wholeness have been presented in an obvious way from outside, whether in the form of rituals and religious ceremonies or in technical and craft practices such as those found in alchemy. Even mythology gives the impression that encounters with God took place long ago 'outwardly' as events that could be given dates: 'gods once roamed upon the Earth', as Hölderlin put it. And tradition has often claimed to pinpoint the exact place where some great divine revelation happened, as though it were possible to be precise about the event and the hallowed spot — if necessary with the help of man-made relics. With such help men sought to experience divinity in the 'here and now'. Superficiality on a wide front!

Without going into the question of what mental images are involved here, it should be said that what is apparently experienced 'outwardly' has its own inward sphere of action, through which it will be perceived by the human psyche. We may recall here the train of thought started by Herbert Silberer, one of Sigmund Freud's unorthodox pupils. Silberer (1882-1923),[1] known as the first psychoanalyst to investigate alchemy, wrote in his *Problems of Mysticism and its Symbols:*

If we develop analytically the symbols appearing in dreams (father, mother, etc.), we have representative examples of *imagos* as psychoanalysts call them, models, the meaning of which will alter according to the way they are looked at, rather as the colour of some minerals changes with the angle at which they are held up to the light. A real father, a real mother, and the experiences that have grown up around them, are the material used in forming these models. They are distinct, but still external entities, whereas later the father, mother and so on, when they appear as symbols, are able to stand for the spiritual potency of the person in question. The psychological power the subject feels resembles a real father; otherwise it would not qualify as a father-figure. We can go so far as to call this power a 'father-image', though this should not tempt us in most cases (not all) to give up the model and take the real outside person for the actual influence. The deepest influence lies *within ourselves* though it is formed from and reacts to people in the outside world.[2]

If we bear in mind the early date of the publication of this observation (1914), then Silberer's opinion is important in that it points in the direction of Jung's work in formulating the concept of the *archetype*. Improvising, Silberer speaks only of 'elementary models' and 'primitive causes'. Such early work enables a psychological understanding to be gained of the mental structure of mystical marriage, *Hieros Gamos, unio mystica,* etc.

For all these and similar symbolic concepts go beyond the scope of everyday human awareness or the powers of comprehension, which are bound up with the Ego (as defined in analytical psychology).

Of course such concepts as marriage, union or communion, joining together, meeting, and so on, are central to human experience. They first constitute and then qualify human existence. Yet at the same time they are recognized as 'not of this world'. For amid all the many divisions within the individual as well as in society, a possibility of becoming whole exists (what is its source?) and with it a chance of salvation. This fundamental opportunity of becoming a complete person extends from the protective gesture of a mother who puts her arm round her child, to the lovers' embrace and even to togetherness in the face of death. And this opportunity is unique, i.e. nothing can take its place. That great communicator, Martin Buber, when he was at an advanced age (in 1947) and had withdrawn more and more into his books, added as a corrective, 'I hear of those who value their solitude, but this is only because there are other people in the world, even if at a distance. I knew nothing about books when I came from my mother's womb and it will be without books that I shall die — a human hand in mine. . .'[3]

In other words, for religious people there is manifested in, with and during these human experiences that Other — the Other, the eternal non-Ego — which allows a human encounter to become an encounter with God, and the erotic-sexual embrace to become mystical marriage. Mircea Eliade went so far as to say:

It was only divine marriage which took place *in illo tempore* [at a time unspecified] that made human sexual union possible. The union of god with goddess takes place in a timeless moment, and eternal present; the union of humans — in so far as it is not ritual union — takes place in secular time. Divine, mythical time is the basis for existing historical time and is its prototype. Everything owes its existence to a divine or semi-divine being. . .[4]

Therefore we agree with Ludwig Feuerbach's opinion, that tangible, earthly experiences or concepts are not projected onto an imaginary heavenly magic-lantern screen, but that it is the other way about; the archetypal symbol, the prototype, provides the ideal form to be translated into reality. Eliade here comes close to Jung's understanding of the archetype, which itself remains invisible, but which because of its effect must be postulated as an underlying 'first cause'. In our case the archetype would represent the union of opposites, standing in a definite relationship with one another and striving away from separation and towards wholeness. A tendency is expressed here which is inherent in 'the structure of the human psyche. This tendency is related to instinct and, like instincts, it indicates the direction a developing organism should follow. The instinct leads to a goal, though the individual in which it operates may not know what the goal is.'[5]

It is a basic fact of human experience that our life and the world we come into contact with can be seen in two ways. First there are the individuals themselves. In essence they are not yet completely whole. They experience themselves more as men *or* as women. Both male and female, however, tend in their respective make-up towards a conjunction in which their opposed qualities will find fulfilment, and yet without losing the tension of opposites — as appears to be the case with hermaphroditism. Only through the power of sexual attraction of opposites can human life occur. Only through man *and* woman can *the* human be created. To adapt Martin Buber, man finds his 'I' in the (sexually opposite) 'You', and 'becoming himself, he speaks of You'. The tension of opposites remains and offers repeated opportunities of becoming a whole person, and what we call being fully alive; for 'holier and more powerful than any written words is an immediate human presence. . . in the magic fulfilment of being together'.[6]

There is a wider aspect of male and female opposites, which concerns the way the human psyche relates to reality. What matters is whether the mind turns towards the inner (psychic) or the outer (material) world. Mutually opposed attitudes emerge — introversion if emphasis is placed on inward objects, extraversion if emphasis is placed on outward objects. The experience of recent decades in particular shows disharmonies that have deeply affected social life; a generation that wears itself out worrying about securing its economic and material well-being naturally neglects specifically human values and earns the criticism of the next generation. Gaining the world through over-emphasized extravert attitudes will be at the expense of loss of soul, both in individuals and society in general. [7] But instead of cultivating an escapist inwardness, it should be a question of 'marrying' introversion in suitable ways with an extravert turning towards the world. We are reminded of the words of Roger Schutz, Prior of the Community of Taizé: 'Act and meditate.' These words reflect the precepts determining the Benedictine approach to life. This consist of harmonizing the *vita activa* of a busy life with the *vita contempliva* of spiritual composure — work and pray!

Another bipolar facet of experience, knowledge of which is much older than modern psychoanalysis, lies in the fact that only part of the human psyche is illuminated by the light of consciousness. And opposed to it is the unconscious, 'the dark side of the soul'. Even if the old Heraclitian maxim — that it was impossible to define the soul — has not lost its validity,[8] because the unconscious is by definition unknowable, if the human being is to mature it is essential to establish a link between the conscious and the unconscious. The Ego, which stands at the centre of the field of consciousness and is the 'number one of personality', is not the complete person. The process of becoming oneself — what C. G. Jung called individuation — is bound up with a creative encounter between the Ego and the unconscious. This 'between' indicates the arena in which the process of becoming whole is played out — mystical marriage, not as an external symbolic event, but as a synthesis *within* people.

The theme of mystical marriage (mostly referred to as *mysterium coniunctionis*) was assigned a central significance in Jung's psychology.[9] Unlike the religious or spiritual historian or the researcher into symbol and myth, it is not the psychologist's function primarily to collect, systematize and interpret the available examples of the subject under investigation. He is concerned with the actual person, who himself produces signs and symbols which serve as a means of expressing his own experience, and as a result of this experience becomes mature — in this case as a result of experience of the union of opposites. This *coniunctio*, the union of opposite poles directed towards the need to become complete, allow the man to become who he *is* and who he can and *should* be, according to his allotted talents. Only with this understanding can the goal be envisaged, i.e. wholeness or the true *incarnation of man,* and also the method of attaining it.

It is nevertheless in the nature of the subject that the historical aims and examples of mystical marriage are of interest to psychological researchers; all the more so since, with the aids to understanding they contain, a person may 'fill out' the practical problems of life and his related unconscious impulses with comparable historical examples. What is suggested is a method developed by Jung to 'enrich' the apparently puzzling products of the unconscious through similarly motivated texts or images from myths, religion or tradition, so that for instance the material of dreams (e.g. a specific situation, shape or number in a dream) is matched by a similar traditional example. The person involved can absorb this inner parallelism, or congruence, causing a shock of recognition. The hitherto incomprehensible motif from the unconscious begins to make sense in a historical context. Finally we find it will establish an awareness of a psychic-spiritual continuity, whether we accept it as a fact or reject it on whatever grounds. Rigid adherence to the everyday Ego consciousness limited by the outside world will all too often furnish 'grounds' for such rejection. This everyday Ego which is at the heart of our daily consciousness — the rationale, with its indispensable analysing and judging functions — is indeed a dominant factor of our consciousness. Also our experiences and perceptions of both outer and inner worlds have to go through this Ego; they have, as it were, to withstand its controlling authority, if they are to exist for us. But the range and depth of this Ego control are limited. The world which can be measured, counted, weighed and manipulated, governs it. The broad — and, since Heraclitus, boundless — field of the unconscious has for long been closed to it, since the Ego-conscious has been unable to decipher the manifestations and signs of the unconscious — as well as those which are psychosomatic. And this function, of deciphering the unconscious, is essential, for it is concerned with:

compensating factors... which are necessary for the self-regulation of the collective psyche. The more one becomes aware of oneself through self-knowledge and its concomitant behaviour, the more the layer of the personal unconscious imposed on the collective unconscious will tend to disappear. Consequently a consciousness arises that is no longer confused in a petty, personally vulnerable Ego-world, but can participate in a wider world of true aims.[10]

New horizons appear. They are the horizons of a reality that stretches beyond the Ego. We are opened up to this dimension of reality, not just in the way that we would be if we were refining the techniques of observation in micro- or macro-physics, but in the sense that we submit to a wholly new way of looking at things in a way that includes the unconscious (the personal as well as the super-personal collective) and it may be initially in the sense of a limited hypothetical acceptance — with verification through experience to follow. And this new way of looking at things, which is part of the psychoanalyst's method, serves a compensatory function, because the conscious is *supplemented* by the unconscious and is consequently made complete. Without putting its competence in question, it is no longer the Ego that dominates but the *Self,* 'as a superior authority over the conscious Ego. It embraces not only the conscious but also the unconscious Ego. It embraces not only the conscious but also the unconscious psyche, and is therefore, so to speak, a personality, something that we are *also*.[11] But are we then already this Self — in the sense that it does not change our human situation, in that we already 'play' certain social roles and our actions are already adjusted to agreed, more or less superficial ends?

The everyday Ego (not to be confused with the 'enduring personality') will be 'socialized', even without special help, by the rules and standards of the prevailing cultural context; it will become adjusted. This Ego (e.g. as parent Ego, teacher, employer, politician, manager, official, etc.) will in its turn influence innumerable others to adjust to the existing society. But questions about the meaning or purpose of life will not be answered in this way. This mass of anonymous Egos, which includes every individual, recognizes only functions and objectives; it is concerned with, and at best achieves, the private, material 'welfare' of individuals, nothing more. And yet the question remains as to where we are going and to what purpose? It often arises in a disturbing way, for example as a mental crisis, with all its known accompanying symptoms: emptiness in spite of material security; inner disharmony even though important personal relationships are 'all right'; loneliness despite a multiplicity of so-called social contacts in the community at large. . .

What are these feelings of insufficiency and conflict other than signs of a yet scarcely perceived Self, which advertises its intention to exist over and above the aims of the everyday, and which presses with authority towards self-realization? Is it not this Self that seeks representation and certainty, with the help of which the individual (other than through the everyday Ego) will be able to find his place in the real world, without feeling lost in the anonymity of a heartless, empty universe?

Signals of this kind do not come out of the blue. Crisis situations may arise at any moment in life. And yet there is a time when the problem of self-realization enters a critical phase, namely, in middle age, when the Ego has already been established in this life, in partnership with colleagues, with economic security and perhaps with provision for our old age, in short, when a basic accommodation with the world has been achieved.

Even then, when the basic problems seem to have been solved, those questions 'Why?', 'To what end?' and 'What next?' make themselves heard almost from nowhere: all uncomfortable issues that we might prefer not to hear, might push aside or 'drown'. If, however, these signals which our mid-life situation gives rise to come from the 'superior authority' of the Self, which until this time has been scarcely noticed, then obviously a moment in life is reached when the Ego must face up to the Self — a moment of real significance.

Life then can be seen, though it may not be clearly expressed like this, as falling into three parts. Middle age is experienced as a turning-point. Rilke's adage says, 'You must change your life!' (Is this not the biblical term of *metánoia*, a fresh start?) Only from middle age onwards will *knowledge* of life's three stages, gained from book learning, become *experience* of life. The period that serves to develop the Ego stretches from birth to middle age. In the middle phase the step from Ego to Self is taken, so that finally one becomes mature enough for the third stage of life, which will find its completion in death.

Analytical psychology differentiates between these three main stages of the evolution of personality. And it also assigns the task of self-discovery to this critical middle phase, with its turning point in life. The symbol of mystical marriage here shows its special anthropological-existential significance, i.e. as a *mysterium coniunctionis* that encompasses a process of transformation and rebirth. The values, standards and aspirations held until now are seen as of only relative importance; they pale into insignificance. The possibility of new experience presents itself. The Ego comes into contact with archetypal reality more closely than before. This archetypal area of the psyche comes to confront the individual human Ego. Here we also have a collective unconscious — we could say a total human consciousness — from which individual cultural epochs have received the principal images and impulses which set their norms and values, as we know them from religious and spiritual history. The metaphor of mystical marriage as a universal human symbol and as a primary means of gaining experience is rooted in this collective unconscious. But how far is this really the case?

Two factors may be pointed out here: on the one hand the existence of the opposites of good and evil, light and darkness; and on the other that of male and female. These opposites play a significant role in the process of becoming oneself (individuation). What is involved on the one hand is to experience the so-called shadow, the dark side of our psyche, in such a way that it will no longer be projected on to external objects (difficult people, unhappy relationships, society, etc.) but will be recognized as belonging to our own psyche. To accept this dark side, to integrate it, to accept the way we are — that should be our aim.

On the other hand, the person seeking to become an individual should be ready to confront what Jung called 'the image of the soul', and what was earlier perceived as external will become as though interiorized within the person's Self. For a man is not only masculine, a woman not only feminine. This implies that in individuation the man should get to know and accept his own unconscious femininity — his *anima*. Something similar should happen for a woman; her conscious (femi-

nine) Ego will be associated with the *animus* as the soul-image
of the opposite sex. In both cases it means finding a real personality, which implies something like a psychical dual sexuality.[12]

An important function is assigned in each case to the image
of the soul. Jung wrote on this point:

> The natural function of the animus (and also of the anima) is to estab-
> lish a connection between the individual consciousness and the col-
> lective unconscious... Animus and anima should function as a
> bridge or a gateway to images of the collective unconscious, just as
> the persona [i.e., the outward, role-acting function] constitutes a kind
> of bridge to the world.[13]

Without going more closely into the special associations of the
'soul image' which are abundantly represented in the literature in both their positive and negative aspects, and to which
there is a practical side, one thing becomes clear: a psychical
reality corresponds to the state of affairs we find in the religio-
historical phenomenon of mystical marriage, a reality which
— as we discuss below — is of no less significance for interpersonal life. Not only is there a relationship between the sexes,
in the form of an 'I-You' relationship or fulfilment in the area
of love and sex; but there is also a relationship to oneself. This
becomes of decisive importance in the second half of life in
which straightforward inter-personal I-You relationships are
established and strengthened. 'Togetherness does not consist
only of outward communication. An inner relationship is the
contact that two people can have from deep within themselves.'[14]

Let us be clear about the psychoanalytical position from
which we start, if we look at this double aspect of two people.
Jung gives us a diagram in which he shows graphically what
has already become his classic 'marriage *quarternio*'. Let us take
first as opposites a woman and a man. Every person is in a relationship with her or his own (unconscious) opposite sexuality, animus or anima. There is a third type of relationship owing
to the fact that communication takes place not only between
the conscious I and You (by look, word or action) but also on
the level of the man's conscious (anima) and that of the woman
(animus). Finally we have to take into account the fact that
impressions can emanate from the unconscious of one person
to the conscious of the other. What happens is that signals are

given which the person concerned is not aware of and cannot control, because they remain unconscious to him or her, but they can still be picked up by the other person from the originator's gestures or expressions.

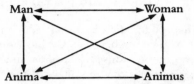

Conscious level: Man ⟷ Woman

Unconscious level: Anima ⟷ Animus

In the accompanying psychotherapeutic process of individuation, it is a question not only of solving the problem of a person's dark side in the sense indicated above, but also of recognizing and controlling projections of the anima or animus on to one's partner of the opposite sex, and indeed for the sake of a 'spiritual marriage', of establishing an inner combination of personality components which will make possible 'an unprojected (sublimated) inner experience'.

What is implied is the unification of the inner opposites within the Self. The old alchemists had an easier task than we do because for them the problem lay, so to speak, in matter, in a retort, where they sought to manufacture the Philosopher's Stone through 'chemical marriage'. We, however, have to carry this out within ourselves and that necessarily goes much deeper under the skin.[15]

The numinous proximity of marriage and death has been referred to repeatedly. And it refers not only to 'mystical death' — the opposite side of *unio mystica* or 'mystical marriage' — as we saw in the case of Irmengard Bardo. The same applies to physical death. When Jung's life was drawing to a close (he died on 6 June 1961), he saw again before his eyes a vision of 'holy marriage' which he had seen once before when death seemed near. This was in May 1959, when a Chilean diplomat, Miguel Serrano, was his guest. The 84-year-old forgot his role as a psychoanalyst and said on the subject of *coniunctio*, as though lost in thought:

There was once a flower, a stone, a crystal, a queen and a king, a castle, a lover and his beloved, somewhere a long, long time ago, on an island in the middle of the ocean, 5,000 years ago. . . Love is like this, the mystical flower of the soul. It is the centre of the Self. . .'

Then he murmured as if in a dream: 'No one understands what I mean. Only a poet can grasp it...'[16]

It becomes clear finally, in the broad biographical context of Jung's life and work, what form, both archetypal and individual, the symbol of mystical marriage can take on for a person in our own time. [17]

13

Paths to the Symbol of
Coniunctio

If we keep in sight the benefits of individuation through psychoanalysis, in which on the one hand problems connected with our shadow side, and on the other those of the animus-anima are worked on, then it would be a good thing if as many people as possible were to undergo 'analysis', and could follow this path to self-fulfilment. We have in mind all those who are not content merely with 'mastery of life', with the ability to conform and with achieving a certain capacity for success. Yet possibilities are very limited. Too seldom does an inner guide come forward — as in the case of Irmengard Bardo — who will act positively and lead to initiation into the *mysterium coniunctionis*.

But it is also clear that psychoanalytic treatment (or more precisely psycho-synthesis) is the exception, not the rule. Jung once referred to a 'school for 40-year-olds', but such a thing is generally unheard of and indeed would hardly be possible, since maturing towards wholeness cannot be taught. And from the start, the much-discussed use of group therapy, aimed at knowing the Self, is subject to narrow limits. As experience has shown, such group therapy, while helpful in itself, is no substitute for an individual's own spiritual activity. What then is to be done?

Much is to be gained if, by middle age at the latest, we take seriously the expressions of our own unconscious, for example, if we pay attention to our dreams. In saying this we are not recommending a kind of do-it-yourself course of psychotherapy, carried out on one's own account. Such a thing would not be without its dangers. But images, especially those that come out of the depths of our own minds, have a message that may be deciphered and if possible acted upon. That is why it is *these* dreams precisely that we remember, while a large part of what we dream every night is not generally capable of being recalled.

But before we talk about deciphering images it is necessary to look at them closely and, as it were, Ego-free; that is, without assumptions and without being influenced by the intellectual Ego as though we already know where the dream is pointing. It is important to pay attention, then, to the mood and emotional character attaching to a dream. We must all acquire individually a basic attitude of open-mindedness as an important precondition for any serious interpretation of the unconscious. Only then may we use the literature of psychology to support our study of dreams as 'God's forgotten language'. But is it really a matter of orthodox study?[1]

Much more important are the unexplained *associations with images and voices from within oneself*. James Hillman, an American follower of Jung, says on this subject that we should immediately 'make friends with a dream'. 'An inner relationship with the unconscious leads. . . to experience of an inner life, of a place where meanings have their home.'[2] It is incontrovertible that established contacts of this kind with our inner self radiate outwards into interpersonal and social areas; for 'human encounters depend on an inner relationship. To communicate closely with another person I must be in close contact with myself.'[3] If we can begin to examine the images and figures of our dreams in the same way as we would look at an unknown, unexpected visitor who knocks at our door and whom we look squarely in the eye, then we have made great progress. Of course, making friends with oneself presupposes a long, patient association. One day we may also be able to 'embrace the wolf' (Luise Rinser) and thereby accept the negative images of our dreams as belonging to us. Usually some transformation precedes this stage, which is closely connected with a new attitude towards our unconscious. It is obvious that confronting the unknown and hitherto unconscious depths of our being will bring an understanding that we never thought possible before.

External symbol-bearers — myths and fairy stories — help the process of coming closer to and making friends with our own femininity (for a man) and our own masculinity (for a woman). The Bible, with its abundance of images of mystical marriage and spiritual betrothal, should not of course be excluded. And it is in fact remarkable that these stories of journeying, transformation, departure, danger and homecoming are not studied much more thoroughly than appears to be the case.[4] Let us now consider fairy stories.

Comparable in many ways to dream-fantasies, fairy tales recount in inexhaustible variety the fate of the human soul, which emerges from insignificance, lack of meaning, apathy, imprisonment or being bewitched, and finds its crowning achievement in the union of those who seek each other consciously or unconsciously because they are 'meant for each other'. And those who just boast about their ability, knowledge or prestige, i.e. Ego-dominated figures, are shown as being basically unable to cope, whereas the youngest, the smallest, the simplest child or the proverbial Cinderella find their way safely to their goal. This goal is reduced to a straightforward happy common denominator with the often-used refrain, 'And they were married and lived happily ever after!' Because in essence the fairy tale is played out beyond the frontiers of reality (in the fairy tale about 'Old Mother Frost', for example, this is symbolized by falling down a well or going through a golden gate) the impossible is possible, even breaking a spell through the transforming and uniting power of love. As Novalis once thoughtfully remarked, 'Perhaps a similar transformation would take place if mankind could extend its love to the evil in the world.'

The marriage of king and queen, which is represented in many different ways in countless fairy tales as the goal and climax of the story, symbolizes the fruitful union of the natural-emotional female side with the male-intellectual. In this union a conjunction of opposites takes place between *Eros* and *Logos*. Hence it is possible for the fairy tale to appeal to us directly, free from any theory connected with psychology or the humanities. And the meaning of the story is clear without any special training, for the obstacles, tests, and expectations are within our own experience. It is surely not by chance that, after a period of neglect or lack of appreciation, the fairy tale today enjoys ever increasing popularity. For what starts out as comfort and encouragement, as the fairy tale's healing power, serves also to support a process of recovery and becoming whole for our divided humanity today.

We have already discussed the theme of mystical marriage, from the metaphorical language of myth through to the language describing religious and spiritual experience. Its mystery is found at the heart of gnosis and mysticism and in every domain of the esoteric, past and present, Eastern and Western. Just as conscious association with dreams and study of fairy tales allows us to approach the great theme of *coniunctio*, so religious fulfilment opens up the world of interpersonal reality. It is this reality of union in which mind and matter, heaven and earth, God and man, are related to one another and are bound up in one another. Religion, especially religious mysticism as a direct experience of God, is consistent with meeting and getting to know the archetype of 'the way' and of *Hieros Gamos*. Admittedly we cannot grasp the full dimensions of mystical marriage by study alone. And yet the fact that interest in mysticism and the esoteric has grown in recent years is evidence of more than just curiosity.[5] All those who know from experience and with a sense of awe, 'the birth of God in the soul' (Master Eckhart) or who praise divine *Sapientia*, the Wisdom of God (Heinrich Seuse) provide testimony that is directly appealing; and it transfers its influence not only from one intellect to another, but also from anima (or animus) to anima, thus acting at the deepest level of the soul. Not for nothing did Martin Luther call the anonymous Frankfurt *Theologia Deutsch* a mystical work which 'originates in the Jordan valley'.[6] And anyone experiencing the change of heart which puts us in touch with our unconscious will understand the richly metaphoric language of Christian mystics, although we should not underestimate the change in our understanding which has taken place since the time of Master Eckhart and Matilda of Magdeburg. A book such as Jakob Böhme's *Christosophia* or 'The Way to Christ', may well be designated as a means of initiation and lead to union with the virgin Sophia.[7]

Everyone who surveys the wide field of written testimony must make his own choice of spiritual literature. Also what is read must first be made one's own, taking into consideration the period and intellectual climate of the particular spiritual-religious work. This is no less true for Eastern and Far Eastern spiritual thought, such as the mystery and practice of *Hieros Gamos* in Tantraism. The dangers of superficial knowledge, especially of these practices, should not be underestimated.

Likewise, caution is also advisable when it comes to choosing a method of meditation; though meditation (provided it does not stop short with words, pictures or symbols) represents a way towards *coniunctio* that no other practice can replace. This 'interiorization' banishes the usually dominant Ego-consciousness to the boundaries of attention, without deadening or destroying it. The field of imaginative imagery can then come through so that the 'inner voice', the voice of tranquillity, can be heard at an inspired level of consciousness. This level will be reached at that stage of intuition at which we can contact or be contacted by the realities of life.[8] The practice of meditation reflects a saying from St Luke's Gospel (2:19) connected with Mary, the mother of Jesus. It was said of her during the events surrounding the birth of Jesus: 'But Mary kept all these things and *pondered* them in her *heart* [my italics]'.

Meditation takes place in the heart, that is, in the depth of one's being, for it is not just a simple mental reflex, not acting with purpose in mind; it is being inwardly receptive. 'Pondering' in one's heart is also therefore not a linear, logical line of reasoning but a *circling round the centre*. It is significant that the original Greek text used a word for 'ponder' (*symballousa*) that clearly reveals its relationship with 'symbol'. It is concerned with symbolizing what is spiritually active, i.e. an inner unifying process. Such a symbolic, inner unifying event becomes the way into that mystery celebrated and glorified 'in a thousand images' as mystical marriage.

Epilogue

'If you want more to read...'

At this point in our examination of the theme of *Hieros Gamos* we might ask, not without a note of scepticism, is there then nothing more precise to be said about mystical marriage and *mysterium coniunctionis* than what little we have attempted to say here? We might well refer to Angelus Silesius (Johann Scheffler). He was perhaps aware of similar questions when he ended his *Cherubinischen Wandersmann (Cherubic Wanderer)*, which overflowed with paradoxes and heretical-sounding assertions, with the lines:

Friend, this is enough. If you want more to read,
Go; yourself become the writing, and yourself the deed.[1]

An answer that can lay claim to validity not only for the *Cherubic Wanderer*! And yet looking for more precise information is justifiable, especially if we are left with the feeling that all the discussion and metaphors are merely circling round a subject that remains somewhat obscure.

It is difficult to disagree. Analytical psychology is familiar with this 'rite' of *circumambulatio*, i.e. circling round the centre.[2] It means, in our context, that intellectual-spiritual realities cannot be tackled head-on. We cannot grasp them by a particular technical trick, for in the end it is not the same as dealing with some external object. The researcher into the theme of human nature is always much more involved with his 'subject'. This is a central problem of psychoanalytical investigation. The enquirer is his own 'subject'. So there is no valid method by which we can unveil once and for all the mystery of the Egyptian goddess of Sais (which is also one of man himself). As Novalis said:

One [man] succeeded; he lifted the veil of the goddess of Sais. But what did he see? He saw — wonder of wonders — himself!

And what can psychology do? Discussing our subject, Jung goes so far as to say bluntly:

The reader should not suppose that psychology is in any position to explain what 'higher sexual union' is, and consequently what *coniunctio* or *psychic pregnancy* are or indeed what a *child of the soul* is. . . Scientific, i.e. impartial, observation that seeks nothing but the truth must beware of over-hasty evaluation or interpretation, for it is faced here with *spiritual matters* which do not suppress intellectual judgement but can dispose of it deceptively.[3]

As for *circumambulatio*, circling round the centre, referred to above, its meaning is more familiar that at first appears. For there is indeed a spontaneous 'at first sight', a once and for all, rather as in a love affair. But there is also the 'time and again' of repeating an action, perhaps in following a custom 'annually repeated' or that is carried out repeatedly in a rite. It is ultimately immaterial whether or not we are in a position to define exactly the likely theological meaning. Religious experience is not dependent on the formulation of theological propositions in logic. Above all, a person who meditates 'knows' what power emanates from the process of circling round the centre. It induces him to go on creating the conditions for spiritual concentration, his inner eye directed towards the central object of meditation, a symbolic event, i.e. a unifying of opposites *par excellence*. Finally, the meditative process may develop into an inner contemplation that dispenses with any object, image or concept. The boundary of *mysterium coniunctionis* is crossed; it can be experienced but not communicated. And what might be communicated, illustrated or explained would have to be 'denied' as unreal, so that what is genuine can be highlighted.

But why not put it in more general terms: is not eurythmy, the beneficial rhythm of sleeping and waking, an individual circling round that mysterious centre that we call life? The conscious ebbs away into the unconscious, the unconscious surges with its driving force towards the mainland of the sunlit conscious, accompanied by unnamed 'blissful desires' which provide a motivation and an impulse:

. . .

Imprisoned need you stay no longer,
In the dark encircling gloom.
Swept aloft by love grown stronger,
Welcomed by your heavenly groom.

. . .

If this joy as yet eludes you,
You must die and be reborn!
On the dark earth it is true,
You are but a guest forlorn.

Notes

Introduction

[1] Jolande Jacobi, *Komplex, Archetypus, Symbol in der Psychologie C. G. Jungs* (Zürich, 1957); Ulrich Mann. *Die Religion in den Religionen* (Stuttgart, 1975), especially p. 60f. For the symbol as signpost to hidden meaning, see particularly Herbert Kessler, *Das Offenbare Geheimnis* (Freiburg, 1977); H. Kessler, *Wissendes Nichtwissen (Telos-Studien* I) (Mannheim, 1977); H. Kessler, *Wegweiser zur Freiheit (Telos-Studien* II) (Mannheim, 1977); H. Kessler, *Bauformen der Esoterik* (Freiburg, 1983).

[2] Karlfried Graf Dürckheim, *Überweltliches Leben in der Welt: Der Sinn der Mündigkeit* (Weilheim, 1968), p. 69f.

1 Aspects of Mystical Marriage in Comparative Religion

[1] For mythical marriage of the gods see especially A Klinz, 'Hieros Gamos', thesis (Halle, 1933).

[2] Erich Neumann, *Amor und Psyche. Deutung eines Märchens. Ein Beitrag zur seelischen Entwicklung des Weiblichen* (1971; Olten-Freiburg, 1979), p. 72. Cf. Marie-Louise von Franz, *Die Erlösung des Weiblichen im Manne* (Frankfurt, 1980).

[3] Ulrich Mann, *Die Religion in den Religionen* (Stuttgart, 1975), p. 220.

[4] Walter F. Otto, *Theophania: Der Geist der altgriechischen Religion* (Hamburg, 1956), p. 24.

[5] Julius Evola, 'Geistige Männlichkeit und erotische Symbolik', in *Antaios* III, p. 283. Cf. J. Evola, *Metaphysik des Sexus* (Stuttgart, 1962).

[6] Among the various editions of the *I Ching: The Book of Changes*, that of Richard Wilhelm (Athana) is recommended. Cf. also Jung's psychoanalytical interpretation in the preface of his *Collected Works*, vol. 11 (Zürich, 1963), p. 633f.

[7] Martin Schönberger, *Verborgener Schlüssel zum Leben* (Munich—Berne, 1973).

[8]   Mircea Eliade, *Das Heilige und das Profane* (Hamburg, 1957), p. 85.

[9]   Julius Schwabe, *Archetyp und Tierkreis* (Basle, 1951), p. 386, suggests that higher marriage recalls the union of sun and moon, 'in which a god is substituted for the sun and a woman for the moon, which was thought to be material, female and earthly. The union of sun and moon takes place only at the time of the new moon. And, according to a belief that spread world-wide, the dark part of the new moon is positioned at the lowest point of the zodiac. Hence *Hieros Gamos*, the mystical marriage of a pair of gods, is according to the old Tauric point of view, an underworld matter, and therefore ritual marriage on a Babylonian tower was a prerequisite for restoring the world to its natural balance. . .' Cf. further Esther Harding, *Frauenmysterien einst und jetzt* (Zürich, 1959).

[10] Eduard Norden, *Das göttliche Kind* (1924; Darmstadt, 1958); more recently Paul Schwarzenau, *Das göttliche Kind* (Stuttgart, 1983).

[11] Erich Neumann, *Ursprungsgeschichte des Bewußtseins* (Zürich, 1949), p. 233.

[12] T. Immoos, 'Die Sonne leuchtet um Mitternacht', in *Aspekte analytischer Psychologie*, ed. Hans Dieckmann, C. A. Meier and H. J. Wilke, for the centenary of Jung's birth (Basle, 1975), p. 290f.

[13] Mircea Eliade, op. cit., p. 86.

[14] M. Eliade, *Das Mysterium der Wiedergeburt: Initiatsriten. ihre kulturelle und religiöse Bedeutung* (Zürich, 1961), p. 196f.

[15] Gerhard Wehr, *Esoterisches Christentum: Aspekte, Impulse, Konsequenzen* (Stuttgart, 1975), p. 95f.

[16] Cf. Albrecht Dieterich, *Eine Mithrasliturgie* (1923; Darmstadt, 1966), p. 125f; Julius Schwabe, op. cit., p. 498f.

[17] Quoted, M. Eliade, *Das Mysterium der Wiedergeburt*, p. 192.

[18] Cf. Albrecht Dieterich, note 16.

[19] See, among others, M. Eliade, *Das Mysterium der Wiedergeburt*, p. 194f.

[20] Rudolf Bultmann, *Das Urchristentum im Rahmen der antiken Religionen* (Reinbeck, 1962), p. 149f.

[21] M. Eliade, *Das Mysterium der Wiedergeburt*, p. 194f.

2 Mystical Marriage in the Old Testament

[1]   Cf. Martin Buber 'Königtum Gottes. Der Glaube der Propheten', in *Werke* vol. II, *Schriften zur Bibel* (Munich—Heidelberg, 1964).

[2]   Heinrich Groß, 'Zur Polarität der Gotteserfahrung in der Prophetie Israels', in *Drei Wege zu dem einen Gott. Glaubenserfahrung in den monotheistischen Religionen*. Ed. A. Falature, J. J. Petuchowski, W. Strolz (Freiburg, 1976), p. 11f.

[3]   Cf. Artur Weiser, 'Das Buch der zwölf kleinen Propheten', in *Das Alte Testament Deutsch*, vol. 24 (Göttingen, 1967), 22f. Cf. also Georg von Gynz-Rekowski, *Symbole des Weiblichen in Gottesbild und Kult des Alten Testaments* (Zürich, 1963).

4   Helmer Ringgren, 'Das Hohelied', in *Das Alte Testament Deutsch*, vol. 16,2 (Göttingen, 1981).

5   Hartmut Schmökel, *Heilige Hochzeit und Hoheslied* (Wiesbaden, 1956).

6   Ibid., p. 119f.

7   Ibid., p. 120.

Appendix: Mandragora, The Fertility Plant

1   Hugo Rahner, *Griechische Mythen in christlicher Deutung* (1957; Darmstadt, 1966), p. 234.

2   Ibid.

3   Honorius Augustodunensis, quoted op. cit., p. 235f.

4   Hildegard von Bingen, *Naturkunde*. Trans. and ed. Peter Riethe (Salzburg, 1974), p. 28.

3 Attitudes to Marriage in the New Testament

1   Walter Schubart, *Religion und Eros* (1941). Ed. Friedrich Seifert (Munich 1966), pp. 134, 137f.

2   Walter Grundmann, *Das Evangelium nach Markus. Theologischer Kommentar zum Neuen Testament*, vol. 2. (East Berlin, 1968), p. 66.

3   Ernst Benz, *Ecclesia Spiritualis* (1934; Darmstadt, 1964); Joachim von Fiore [Gioacchino of Fiore], *Das Reich des Heiligen Geistes*. Ed. Alfons Rosenberg (Bietigheim, 1977); Gerhard Wehr, *Esoterisches Christentum* (Stuttgart, 1975), p. 160f.

4   See especially Rudolf Schnackenburg, *Das Johannes-evangelium. Herders Theologischer Kommentar zum Neuen Testament*, vol IV, 1 (Freiburg, 1967), p. 328f.

5   Wilhelm Fraenger, *Die Hochzeit zu Kana: Ein Dokument semitischer Gnosis bei Hieronymus Bosch*. (Berlin, 1950); W. Fraenger, *Hierony mus Bosch* (Dresden-Gütersloh, 1975), 145f.

6   Emil Bock, *Die Drei Jahre (Beiträge zur Geistesgeschichte der Menschheit,* 2nd series, vol. III) (Stuttgart, 1949), p. 60f.

7   Arthur Schutt, *Das Johannes-Erangelium als Offenbarung des kosmischen Christus* (Remagen, 1965), p.92.

8   Rudolf Schnackenburg, op. cit., p. 455.

9   Wilhelm Stählin, *Predigthilfen*. Vol. I: *Evangelien* (Kassel, 1967), p. 376.

10 Max Zerwick, *Der Brief an die Epheser. Geistliche Schriftlesung*, vol. 10, (Düsseldorf, 1963), p. 168.

11 Franz Mussner, *Christus, das All und die Kirche. Studien zur Theologie des Epheserbriefs* (Trier, 1968), p. 150.

12 Ernst Lohmeyer, *Die Offenbarung des Johannes. Handbuch zum Neuen Testament*, vol. 16 (Tübingen, 1953), p. 98.

13 Virgil, *Fourth Eclogue*.

14 Cf. Eduard Lohse, *Die Offenbarung des Johannes. Das Neue Testament*

146 THE MYSTICAL MARRIAGE

Deutsch, vol. 11 (Göttingen, 1966); Ernst Lohmeyer, op. cit; Emil Bock, *Apokalypse, Betrachtungen über die Offenbarung des Johannes* (Stuttgart, 1952).

[15] Rudolf Schnackenburg, *Die Kirche im Neuen Testament. (Quaestiones Disputatae 14)* (Freiburg, 1961), p.105.

[16] Emil Bock, *Apokalypse* (Stuttgart, 1952), p. 260.

[17] Ibid., p. 233.

4 Gnostic Mysteries

[1] St Clement of Alexandria, *Excerpta ex Theodoto* § 78, quoted, Werner Foerster, *Die Gnosis*, vol. I. (Bibliothek der Alten Welt) (Zürich, 1969), p. 17f.

[2] Werner Foerster, op. cit., p. 8.

[3] Cf. Gilles Quispel, *Gnosis als Weltreligion* (1951; Zürich, 1972).

[4] Hans Leisegang, *Der Heilige Geist. Das Wesen und Werden der mystisch-intuitiven Erkenntnis in der Philosophie und Religion der Griechen*, vol. I,1 (1919; Darmstadt, 1967), p. 234.

[5] Philo, *De somniis*, I, 200, quoted Hans Leisegang, *Die Gnosis* (1921; Stuttgart, 1941), p. 32.

[6] Irenaeus, *Adv. haer.* I, 21, 3, quoted Robert Haardt, *Die Gnosis: Wesen und Zeugnisse* (Salzburg, 1967), p. 134.

[7] Kurt Rudolph, *Die Gnosis. Wesen und Geschichte einer spätantiken Religion* (Leipzig, 1977, Göttingen, 1978), p.251.

[8] Cited Hans Leisegang, *Die Gnosis* (Stuttgart, 1941) p. 30f; Cf. *Die Gnosis* I (note 1 above), p. 441f.

[9] Wilhelm Bousset, *Kyrios Christos. Geschichte des Christusglaubens von den Anfängen des Christentums bis Irenäus* (1913; Göttingen, 1965), p. 205. Cf. ibid., *Hautprobleme der Gnosis* (Göttingen, 1907), p. 267f.

[10] Kurt Rudolph, op. cit., p. 252.

[11] Acts of Philip, 67f.

[12] 'Die Exegese über die Seele', in *Gnosis* II, ed. Carl Andresen (Zürich, 1971), p. 131.

[13] Hans Jonas, *Gnosis und spätantiker Geist*, I, 3. rev. ed. (Göttingen, 1964), p. 192f.

[14] Cf. among others Walter Bauer, *Rechtgläubigkeit und Ketzerei im ältesten Christentum* (1934; Tübingen, 1963) Gerhard Wehr, *Esoterisches Christentum* (Stuttgart, 1975) and *Auf den Spuren urchristlicher Ketzer: Christliche Gnosis und heutiges Bewußtsein* (Schaffhausen, 1983).

5 Conjugal Kabbalistic Mysteries

[1] *Sefer ha-Zohar*, III, 296 a; cf. Siegfried Hurwitz, 'Archetypische Motive in der chassidischen Mystik', in *Zeitlose Dokumente der Seele*, ed. C. A. Meier (Studien aus dem C. G. Jung-Institut III) (Zürich, 1952), p. 175.

2   *Sefer ha-Zohar*, III 296 a-b; Cf. *Der Sohar*. from the original text ed.
    by Ernst Müller (Vienna, 1932), p. 390.

3   As an introduction, Ernst Müller, *Der Sohar und seine Lehre*, 3rd ed.
    (Zürich, 1959); Gershom Scholem, *Die jüdische Mystik in ihren Haupt-
    strömungen* (Frankfurt, 1957, rev. ed.).

4   Gershom Scholem, *Von der mystischen Gestalt der Gottheit Studien zu
    Grundbegriffen der Kabbala* (Zürich, 1962), p. 178.

5   Gerhard Wehr, 'Baal-Schem-Tow', in *Die Großen der Weltgeschichte*,
    ed. Kurt Fassmann (Zürich, 1975), vol. VI, pp. 456-65; and Wehr,
    Der Chassidismus: Mysterium und spirituelle Lebenspraxis (Freiburg,
    1978).

6   Alexandre Safran, *Die Kabbala* (Berne—Munich 1966), p. 182.

7   *Sefer ha-Zohar*, III, 29 a; cf. Hurwitz, op. cit., p. 173.

8   Ibid., III, 93 a; cf. Hurwitz, op. cit., p. 174.

9   Gershom Scholem, *Von der mystischen Gestalt der Gottheit*, p. 180.

10 G. Scholem, *Zur Kabbala und ihrer Symbolik* (Zürich, 1960), p. 177.

11 Ibid., p. 185.

12 Ibid., p. 185f.

13 Ibid., p. 188f.

14 Ibid., p. 190f; see also H. J. Schoeps ed. *Jüdische Geisteswelt: Zeug-
    nisse aus zwei Jahrtausenden* (Darmstadt, 1953), p. 125f.

15 *Sefer ha-Zohar*, I, 49 b-50 a, quoted in Ernst Müller, op. cit., p. 123.

16 *Sefer ha-Zohar*, II, 81 a, b, in Müller, op. cit., p. 125. Cf. further Georg
    Langer, *Liebesmystik der Kabbala* (Munich—Planegg, 1956);
    Friedrich Weinreb, *Der göttliche Bauplan der Welt* (Zürich, 1971), pp.
    112f., 118f.

6 Mystical Marriage

1   *Theologia Deutsch. Eine Grundschrift deutscher Mystik*. Ed., with an
    introduction by Gerhard Wehr (Frieburg, 1980), p. 25.

2   Ibid., p. 26.

3   Cf. Gerhard Wehr, *Deutsche Mystik. Gestalten und Zeugnisse religiöser
    Erfahrung von Meister Eckhart bis zur Reformationszeit* (Gütersloh, 1980)
    (GTB 365), p. 80f.

4   *Theologia Deutsch*, p. 48.

5   Cf. Gerhard Wehr, *Esoterisches Christentum* (Stuttgart, 1975), pp.
    176-91.

6   'Symeon, der neue Theologe: Aus den Liebesgesängen an Gott',
    Ekstatische Konfessionen, collected by Martin Buber (Leipzig, 1921),
    p. 55.

7   Evelyn Underhill, *Mystik. Eine Studie über die Natur und Entwick-
    lung des religiösen Bewußseins im Menschen* (1928); Bietigheim n.d., p.
    180.

8   Friedrich Heiler, *Das Gebet: Eine religionsgeschichtliche und religions-
    psychologische Untersuchung* (1918; Munich 1923), p. 331f.

9   Ibid., p. 243.
10 St Bernard of Clairvaux, *Sermones in Cantica Canticorum*, VII, cited
    E. Underhill, op. cit., p. 181f.
11 St Bernard of Clairvaux, *Sermones* 83, in his *Die Botschaft der Freude*.
    Chosen and introduced by Jean Leclercq (Zürich, 1977) p. 153
    (Klassiker der Meditation).
12 St Bernard of Clairvaux in *Christliche Geisteswelt: Die Welt der Mys-*
    tik, ed. Walther Tritsch (Baden-Baden, 1957), p. 99f.
13 Matilda of Magdeburg in ibid., p. 142f.
14 Christina Ebner, in ibid., p. 144.
15 Jan van Ruysbroeck, *Die Zierde der geistlichen Hochzeit*. Ed. and tr.
    by Friedrich Markus Huebner (Leipzig, 1924), p. 339.
16 Ibid., p. 341. Cf. Bernhard Fraling, *Der Mensch vor dem Geheimnis*
    Gottes. Untersuchungen zur geistlichen Lehre Jan van Ruusbroec (Würz-
    burg, 1967).
17 Reinhard Schwarz, 'Die Brautmystik Martin Luthers', in *Zeitwende*,
    52, 4/1981, p. 193f. See also Gerhard Wehr, *Martin Luther — Mys-*
    tische Erfahrung und christliche Freiheit (Schaffhausen, 1982).
18 Martin Luther: Sermon, 14 October 1537 (WA 22, 335, 23ff), cited,
    R. Schwarz, op. cit., p. 196.
19 Martin Luther, cited, op. cit., p. 203.
20 Alois Haas: *Sermo mysticus. Studien zu Theologie und Sprache der deut-*
    schen Mystik. (Freiburg/Switzerland, 1979), p. 112. See also Louis
    Cognet, *Gottes Geburt in der Seele, Einführung in die deutsche Mystik*
    (Freiburg, 1980).
21 St Teresa of Avila, *Seelenburg*, cited, Heinrich Dumoulin, *Östliche*
    Meditation und christliche Mystik (Freiburg, 1966), p. 56; St Teresa of
    Avila, *Die innere Burg* (Stuttgart, 1966; Zürich, 1979); St Teresa of
    Avila, *Gotteserfahrung und Weg in die Welt*. Ed., introduced and tr.
    by Ulrich Dobhan (Olten-Freiburg, 1979. See also Josef Sudbrack,
    Erfahrung einer Liebe. Teresa von Avilas Mystik als Begegnung mit Gott
    (Freiburg, 1979).

7 Jakob Böhme and Marriage with the Divine Sophia

1   Walter Delius, *Geschichte der Marienfrömmigkeit* (Munich—Basle,
    1963); Gerhard Wehr, *Martin Luther — Mystische Erfahrung und christ-*
    liche Freiheit (Schaffhausen, 1982).
2   Delius, op. cit., p. 218.
3   For an introduction see Gerhard Wehr, *Jakob Böhme in Selbstzeug-*
    nissen und Bilddokumenten (Reinbek, 1971 (Lit.)), *Jakob Böhme: Die*
    Morgenröte bricht an. Zeugnisse der Naturfrömmigkeit und der Christus-
    erkenntnis. Ed. and introduced by Gerhard Wehr (Freiburg, 1983)
    (Herderbücherei 1 077). The annotated student edition is also a
    good introduction to Böhme's work. (Freiburg, 1975f). Ibid., *Vom*
    übersinnlichen Leben (Stuttgart, 1986).

[4] Jakob Böhme, 'Zweite Schutzschrift wider Balthasar Tilke', p. 296f, in *Jakob Böhme — Geistige Schau und Christuserkenntnis*, p. 76.

[5] Jakob Böhme, *Aurora*, Ch. 19, 8-15, quoted, ibid., p. 63.

[6] Ernst Benz, 'Sophia Visionen des Westens, in *The Ecumenical World of Orthodox Civilisation*, ed. Andrew Blane (Mouton, 1973), p. 121f.; Walter Nigg, *Drei große Zeichen: Elias, Hiob, Sophia* (Olten, 1972).

[7] St Augustine, and particularly St Basil the Great, quoted in Gottfried Arnold, *Das Geheimnis der göttlichen Sophia* (Leipzig, 1700; Stuttgart, 1963), p. 119.

[8] Cf. the Appendix to this chapter, 'The Myth of Androgyny, pp. 85-90.

[9] Jakob Böhme, *Mysterium Magnum* (1623), 18, 2.

[10] Ibid., p. 18,6f.

[11] Böhme, *Vom dreifachen Leben des Menschen* (1620), 9, 109.

[12] Böhme, *Mysterium Magnum* 19,7.

[13] Böhme, *Von wahrer Buße*, 1,34.

[14] Franz von Baader in *Bayerische Annalen* (1834) quoted, Gerhard Wehr, *Franz von Baader. Zur Reintegration des Menschen in Religion, Natur und Erotik* (Freiburg, 1980), p. 78. Bernhard Sill, *Androgynie und Geschlechtsdifferenz nach F. von Baader* (Regensburg, 1986).

[15] First completely new edition in 2 vols Böhme's *Theosophische Sendbriefe* are illuminating here. (Freiburg, 1980).

[16] Böhme, *Zweite Schutzschrift wider Balthasar Tilke* (1621), § 72.

[17] Ibid., § 74f.

[18] Böhme, *Von den drei Prinzipien göttlichen Wesens* (1619), 15, 15.

[19] Böhme, *Von wahrer Buße* I, 25, see *Christosophia* (Freiberg, 1975), p. 34.

[20] Ibid., I, 29.

[21] Ernst Benz, *Der vollkommene Mensch nach Jakob Böhme* (Stuttgart, 1937), p. 120. Cf. further especially Eberhard Pältz, *Jakob Böhmes Hermeneutik, Geschichtsverständnis und Sozialethik* (Habilitationsschrift) (Jena, 1961); Arthur Schult, *Maria-Sophia. Das Ewig Weibliche in Gott, Mensch und Kosmos* (Bietigheim, 1960) p. 58f.

[22] Böhme, *Von wahrer Buße*, I, 32.

Appendix: The Myth of Androgyny

[1] Nikolai Berdyayev, *Die Bestimmung des Menschen*, quoted, Ernst Benz, *Adam: Der Mythus vom Urmenschen* (Munich—Planegg, 1955) p. 7.

[2] Julius Evola, *Metaphysik des Sexus* (Stuttgart, 1962), p. 83.

[3] June Singer, *Nur Frau — nur Mann? Wir sind auf beides angelegt* (Munich, 1981), p. 18.

[4] Ibid. June Singer has tried to clarify the terms hermaphrodite, bisexual and androgynous. Cf. also Sukie Colegrave, *Yin und Yang. Die Kräfte des Weiblichen und des Männlichen — Spannung und Aus-*

gleich zwischen den beiden Polen des Seins (Berne—Munich, 1979);
Gerhard Wehr, *Der Urmensch und der Mensch der Zukunft. Das Andro-*
gynproblem männlich-weiblicher Ganzheit im Lichte der Anthroposophie
Rudolf Steiners. (Freiburg, 1964; 1980).

[5] Mircea Eliade, *Mephistopheles and the Androgyne*, cited, June Singer
op. cit., p. 31f. Cf. further Mircea Eliade, *Das Mysterium der Wieder-*
geburt (Zürich, 1961).

[6] C. G. Jung, 'Der Hermaphroditismus des Kindes', in *Gesammelte*
Werke, 9, Part I, p. 188.

[7] Cf. J. Jervell, *Imago dei. Genesis 1,26f. im Spätjudentum, in der Gnosis*
und in den paulinischen Briefen (Göttingen, 1960); Hans Martin
Schenke: *Der Gott 'Mensch' in der Gnosis: Ein religions geschichtlicher*
Beitrag zur Diskussion über die paulinische Anschauung von der Kirche
als Leib Christi (Göttingen, 1962).

[8] Cf. Ernst Michel, *Ehe: Eine Anthropologie der Geschlechtsgemeinschaft*
(Stuttgart, 1948; 1950).

[9] As an introduction, see Gerhard Wehr, *Friedrich Christoph Oetinger:*
Theosoph, Alchymist, Kabbalist (Freiburg, 1978) (Fermenta cognitionis
3); refers to *Alle Weisheit ist von Gott. Gestalten und Wirkungen christ-*
licher Theosophie (Oetinger und Hahn, among others) (Gütersloh,
1980) (Gütersloher Taschenbuch 1016).

[10] Gerhard Wehr, *Saint-Martin: Das Abenteuer des 'Unbekannten*
Philosophen' auf der Suche nach dem Geist (Freiburg, 1980) (Fermenta
cognitionis 9).

[11] Willi Lambert, *Franz von Baaders Philosophie des Gebets; Ein Grun-*
driss seines Denkens (Innsbruck, 1978), Gerhard Wehr, *Franz von*
Baader. Zur Reintegration des Menschen in Religion, Natur und Erotik
(Freiburg, 1980) (Fermenta cognitionis 11).

[12] Referred to in Ernst Benz, *Adam: Der Mythus vom Urmenschen*
(Munich—Planegg, 1955).

[13] Gerhard Wehr, *Der Urmensch und der Mensch der Zukunft. Das Andro-*
gynproblem männlich-weiblicher Ganzheit im Lichte der Anthroposophie
Rudolf Steiners (Freiburg, 1964; 1980).

[14] Rudolf Steiner, *Aus der Akasha-Chronik* (1904). Complete edition
(Dornach, 1955), p. 78.

8 A Discussion of Alchemy

[1] Cf. Erich Neumann, *Ursprungsgeschichte des Bewußtseins* (Zürich,
1949). See also Jean Gebser, *Ursprung und Gegenwart* I/II (Stuttgart,
1949; 1953); Hans Erhard Lauer, *Geschichte als Stufengang der Mensch-*
heit I/III (Freiburg, 1956-61); Franz Zwilgmeyer, *Stufen des Ich:*
Bewußtseinsentwicklung der Menschheit in Gesellschaft und Kultur (Fellbach, 1981).

[2] C. G. Jung, 'Der Geist Mercurius', in *Gesammelte Werke*, 13, p. 255.

[3] Mircea Eliade, *Schmiede und Alchemisten* (Stuttgart, n.d. (1960)), p. 43.

[4] Jung, *Psychologie und Alchemie* (Zürich, 1952), p. 320 (now in *Gesammelte Werke*, 12).

[5] Cf. Rolf Christian Zimmermann, *Das Weltbild des jungen Goethe: Studien zur hermetischen Tradition des deutschen 18. Jahrhunderts*. vol. I, (Munich, 1969); vol. II, (Munich, 1979).

[6] Herbert Silberer, *Probleme der Mystik und Ihrer Symbolik* (Vienna, 1914; Darmstadt, 1961).

[7] Jakob Böhme, *Von der Menschwerdung Jesu Christi*, I, 4, 10 (annotated new edition, Freiburg, 1978).

[8] Angelus Silesius, *Der Cherubinische Wandersmann* (Schaffhausen, 1977); *Der Himmel ist in dir* (Cologne, 1982) (Klassiker der Meditation).

[9] Böhme, *De signatura rerum*, 7, 73; 77f.

[10] Jung, *Psychologie und Alchemie*, p. 575.

[11] Gerhard Dorn (Dorneus), cited Jung, *Psychologie und Alchemie*, p. 351. Cf. G. Goldschmidt, 'Von der Polarität in der antiken Alchemie', in *Antaios*, VII, pp. 149-55.

[12] Heinrich Schipperges, 'Strukturen und Prozesse alchimistischer Überlieferungen', in Emil Ploss et al., *Alchimia: Ideologie und Technologie* (Munich, 1970), p. 91f.

9 The Chemical Marriage of Christian Rosenkreutz

[1] Richard van Dülmen, *Die Utopie einer christlichen Gesellschaft: Johann Valentin Andreae*, Part I (Stuttgart, 1978). As an introduction, see Gerhard Wehr, *Alle Weisheit ist von Gott: Gestalten und Wirkungen christlicher Theosophie* (Gütersloh, 1980) (Gütersloher Taschenbuch 1016).

[2] The complete, standardized text of the Rosenkreutz work is in *Die Bruderschaft der Rosenkreuzer*, ed. and introduced by Gerhard Wehr (Cologne, 1984) (Diederich's Gelbe Reihe, 53).

[3] Gerhard Wehr, *Christian Rosenkreuz* (Freiburg, 1980) (Fermenta cognitionis 10).

[4] Alfons Rosenberg, 'Der Rosenkreuzer J. V. Andreae', in *Die Chymische Hochzeit Christiani Rosenkreutz* (Munich-Planegg, 1957), p. 44.

[5] Rudolf Steiner, 'Die Chymische Hochzeit des Christian Rosenkreuz'. in R. Steiner, *Philosophie und Anthroposophie. Gesammelte Aufsätze 1904-18* (Dornach, 1965), p. 341.

[6] Gerhard Wehr's series, 'Fermenta cognitionis' (on, among others, Paracelsus, Valentin Weigel, Jakob Böhme, F. Chr. Oetinger, Christian Rosenkreutz, Saint-Martin, Franz von Baader, Novalis, Rudolf Steiner), started by Aurum Verlag (Freiburg, 1978f), now obtainable from the author, seeks to satisfy the driving force.

[7] C. G. Jung's letter of 25 April 1955 in *Briefe*, II, p. 481f.

10 'Christ and Sophie': The Mysterium Coniunctionis in the Work of Novalis

1. Cf. the comprehensive account, with accompanying selected texts from the poetry and philosophical writing: *Novalis: Der Dichter und Denker als Christuszeuge*. ed. Gerhard Wehr (Schaffhausen, 1976) (Zeugnisse christlicher Esoterik, 1).
2. Gerhard Wehr, *Novalis: Ein Meister christlicher Einweihung* (Freiburg, 1980) (Fermenta cognitionis 8).
3. Martin Beheim-Schwarzbach, *Novalis — Friedrich von Hardenberg*. (Hamburg, 1948), p. 65.
4. Friedrich Hiebel, *Novalis*, 2nd rev. ed. (Berne-Munich, 1972), p. 360.

11 Mystical Marriage in Modern Times: A Report

1. Apart from a brief mention in a radio broadcast, the author first reported on this in the Freiburg monthly journal, *Esotera*, 31st year, 1980, vol. 4, pp. 311-17. To this was added a short report on her experience by Irmengard Bardo, 'Experiences of carrying out "automatic writing"', ibid., pp. 318-20.
2. Care has been taken to preserve the material that has been collected since 1946, to make it accessible for research purposes. This consists of the original 'writing' and the subsequent typewritten transcription undertaken by Irmengard Bardo herself, numerous MSS with explanations and interpretations, and also many cassettes on which conversations are recorded. Finally there is correspondence with a small circle of doctors, psychoanalysts and parapsychologists.
3. The quotations from the 'automatic' writing and Frau Bardo's reports are reproduced with her kind permission. Apart from the short item mentioned in note 1 above, they are all only in MS or typescript form.
4. Irmengard Bardo's experience of mystical death was not typical, since she achieved an inner readiness to let go; however, no inner shock, no 'death of old Adam', was reported in any form.
5. Irmengard Bardo, 'Erfahrungen. . .' in *Esotera* (1980, vol. 4), p. 317.

12 Towards Self-Realization through Psychoanalysis

1. On Herbert Silberer cf. Paul Roazen, *Sigmund Freud und sein Kreis: Eine biographische Geschichte der Psychoanalyse* (Bergisch-Gladbach, 1976), p. 331f.
2. Herbert Silberer, *Probleme der Mystik und ihrer Symbolik* (Vienna, 1914; Darmstadt, 1961), p. 160.
3. Martin Buber, *Bücher und Menschen* (1947); in Buber, *Hinweise* (Zürich, 1953), p. 9.
4. Mircea Eliade, *Das Heilige und das Profane: Vom Wesen Des Religiösen* (Hamburg, 1957), p. 52 (c. 31).

5 Esther Harding, *Das Geheimnis der Seele: Ursprung und Ziel der psychischen Energie* (1948; Zürich, n.d.) 4th ed., p. 352.
6 Martin Buber, *Leistung und Dasein* (1914); in *Hinweise*, op. cit., p. 12f.
7 Wilhelm Bitter, *Der Verlust der Seele: Ein Psychotherapeut analysiert die moderne Gesellschaft* (Freiburg, 1969) (Herderbücherei 333).
8 Heraclitus, 'It is impossible for you to trace the boundaries of the soul, whatever paths you tread; its meaning (*logos*) is so deep.' (Fragment 45).
9 Reference should be made especially to Jung's late work, e.g. *Psychologie und Alchemie* (1944); *Psychologie der Übertragung* (1946; 1963); *Mysterium Coniunctionis* I/II (1954; 1968).
10 C. G. Jung, Die Beziehungen zwischen dem Ich und dem Unbewussten', in *Gesammelte Werke*, 7, 196.
11 Ibid., p. 195.
12 Emma Jung, *Animus und Anima* (Zürich, 1967).
13 C. G. Jung in an unpublished seminar paper (1925), cited. Cf. among others C. G. Jung, *Erinnerungen, Träume, Gedanken* (Zürich, 1962), p. 409.
14 James Hillman, *Die Begegnung mit sich selbst: Psychologie und Religion* (Stuttgart, 1969), p. 38.
15 Marie-Louise von Franz, *C. G. Jung: Sein Mythos in unserer Zeit* (Frauenfeld, 1972), p. 278f.
16 Miguel Serrano, *Meine Begegnungen mit C. G. Jung und Hermann Hesse in visionärer Schau* (Zürich, 1968), p. 81.
17 Set out in detail in the biography by Gerhard Wehr, *C. G. Jung: Leben, Werk, Wirkung* (Munich, 1985).

13 Paths to the Symbol of Coniunctio

1 Helmut Hark, *Der Traum als Gottes vergessene Sprache: Symbolpsychologische Deutung biblischer und heutiger Träume* (Olten, 1982); H. Hark, *Träume als Ratgeber* (Reinbek, 1986).
2 James Hillman, *Die Begegnung mit sich selbst* (Stuttgart, 1969), p. 62.
3 Ibid., p. 37.
4 Hildegunde Wöller, 'Selbstverwirklichung – Thema der Bibel?' in *Grenzen in Seelsorge und Psychotherapie*, ed. P. M. Pflüger (Fellbach, 1982), p. 90f.
5 Ingrid Riedel (ed.), *Der unverbrauchte Gott: Neue Wege der Religiosität* (Berne, 1976); Gerd-Klaus Kaltenbrunner (ed.), *Die Suche nach dem anderen Zustand: Wiederkehr der Mystik?* (Freiburg 1975) (Herderbücherei Initiative 15). G. K. Kaltenbrunner, *Wissende, Verschwiegene, Eingeweihte. Hinführung zur Esoterik* (Freiburg, 1981) (Herderbücherei Initiative 42); Hans Jürgen Baden, *Das Erlebnis Gottes: Was bedeutet uns die Erfahrung der Mystik?* (Freiburg, 1981).
6 *Theologia Deutsch*. Ed. and introduced by Gerhard Wehr (Freiburg, 1980).

[7] Jakob Böhme, *Christosophia: Ein christlicher Einweihungsweg* (Freiburg, 1975); Böhme, *Vom übersinnlichen Leben* (Ogham-Bücherei-28) (Stuttgart, 1986).

[8] In more detail in Gerhard Wehr, *Der innere Weg: Anthroposophische Erkenntnis und meditative Praxis* (Reinbek, 1983).

Epilogue: 'If you want more to read...'

[1] Angelus Silesius, *Der Cherubinische Wandersmann* (Schaffhausen, 1977) complete edition; Angelus Silesius, *Der Himmel ist in dir* (Zürich-Cologne, 1982) (Klassiker der Meditation).

[2] Cf. Erich Neumann, *Umkreisung der Mitte: Aufsätze zur Tiefenpsychologie der Kultur* I/III (Zürich, 1953).

[3] C. G. Jung, 'Die Psychologie der Übertragung', in *Gesammelte Werke*, 16, 271.

Index

THE ESSENCE OF SPIRITUAL PHILOSOPHY

HARIDAS CHAUDHURI

This book brings together selections from the writings and lectures of the distinguished philosopher and spiritual teacher Haridas Chaudhuri. Weaving together Eastern and Western thought, Dr Chaudhuri, using his own special philosophical perspective, shows how an evolution of consciousness is taking place on both individual and collective levels towards a state of awareness which truly integrates spirit within matter on all levels of existence.

Human beings are by nature spiritual, and the fulfilment of our spiritual potential should be the principal work in the life of each person so that wholeness, balance, harmony and integration can help us toward the creation of the kingdom of heaven on earth. Dr Chaudhuri's teachings provide valuable guidance as to how this fulfilment may be achieved, ranging over such diverse subjects as the problems of faith, free will and determinism, and the nature and practice of meditation. His work also includes modern theories of depth psychology as well as ancient mystical traditions.

The challenge of this book — as of the era to come — is to be aware of, assimilate, respond to and assist in creating this potential dynamic aga of synthesis, allowing the deepest dreams of mankind to come true.